ENDORSEMEN

FEAR! breaks down what it takes to become successful under highly stressful circumstances: mental and physical practice, balancing risk versus outcomes and push way beyond your limits.

—Tommy Caldwell
legendary rock climber and author of The Push.

Despite the obvious physical demands, climbing is even more a rigorous and challenging mental endeavor—after all, the hands and feet are simply an extension of a climber's thoughts and will. In her fascinating book, **FEAR!,** Roanne van Voorst explores the highly distinct thought processes and belief systems of some of the world's top climbers. **FEAR!** Is a uniquely compelling, inspiring, and enlightening read from which you can glean useful mental techniques and strategies for overcoming many of life's challenges and summiting your personal "Everest".

—Eric Hörst
author of the international best-seller Training For Climbing

Climbing is a great metaphor for life. It teaches you both great successes and the lowest lows. In **FEAR!,** some of the worlds' best climbers reflect on what success is worth - and how it can be accomplished.

—Steve House
alpinist, founder of Uphill Athlete.

The realm of fear is intertwined between mind and soul, science and art, calculation and passion. Fear is not a switch you can turn off, but it is something you can manage. This book is a fascinating insight into the minds of some of the world's greatest "fear managers". I felt strangely comforted knowing that even the best of us get scared – comfort in the knowledge that these legends were not born fearless.

—Robbie Philips

professional climber, coach, public speaker.

FEAR!

**EXTREME ATHLETES ON HOW TO REACH
YOUR HIGHEST GOALS
AND OVERCOME STRESS AND SELF-DOUBT**

Roanne van Voorst (PhD)

Published by Motivational Press, Inc.
1777 Aurora Road
Melbourne, Florida, 32935
www.MotivationalPress.com

Copyright 2017 © by Roanne van Voorst
All Rights Reserved

No part of this book may be reproduced or transmitted in any form by any means: graphic, electronic, or mechanical, including photocopying, recording, taping or by any information storage or retrieval system without permission, in writing, from the authors, except for the inclusion of brief quotations in a review, article, book, or academic paper. The authors and publisher of this book and the associated materials have used their best efforts in preparing this material. The authors and publisher make no representations or warranties with respect to accuracy, applicability, fitness or completeness of the contents of this material. They disclaim any warranties expressed or implied, merchantability, or fitness for any particular purpose. The authors and publisher shall in no event be held liable for any loss or other damages, including but not limited to special, incidental, consequential, or other damages. If you have any questions or concerns, the advice of a competent professional should be sought.

Manufactured in the United States of America.

ISBN: 978-1-62865-436-3

CONTENTS

ENDORSEMENTS.. 1
INTRODUCTION 7
CHAPTER 1 12
    ALAIN ROBERT
    'BE PASSIONATELY DISCIPLINED'
CHAPTER 2 23
    ALEX HONNOLD
    'FEAR IS A REACTION TO THE PAST. DON'T LET IT DETERMINE THE FUTURE.'
CHAPTER 3 34
    ALEXANDER SCHULZ
    'LET GO OF EVERYTHING THAT YOU DO NOT NEED'
CHAPTER 4 44
    ARNO ILGNER
    'BECOME AWARE OF YOUR 'NOW-MOTIVATION' AND FOCUS ON THE LEARNING PROCESS'
CHAPTER 5 54
    CATHERINE DESTIVELLE
    'GATHER A TEAM OF EXPERTS AROUND YOU'
CHAPTER 6 66
    CEDRIC DUMONT
    'DEVELOP A STATE OF HYPER-AWARENESS'
CHAPTER 7 75
    DAN GOODWIN
    'DARE TO THINK NEGATIVELY'
CHAPTER 8 86
    DON MCGRATH
    'PERFORM AN ANALYSIS OF YOUR FEAR'

CHAPTER 9 .... **94**
    EDURNE PASABAN
    'LET YOURSELF BE GUIDED BY FEAR'

CHAPTER 10 .... **104**
    JORG VERHOEVEN
    'APPROACH YOUR GOAL SYSTEMATICALLY'

CHAPTER 11 .... **113**
    HAZEL FINDLAY
    'STRENGTHEN YOUR FEAR-MUSCLE'

CHAPTER 12 .... **122**
    LYNN HILL
    'STOP. ACCEPT. REFRESH YOUR MIND. CONTINUE'

CHAPTER 13 .... **133**
    MARTIN FICKWEILER
    'DARE TO TAKE UNTRODDEN PATHS'

CHAPTER 14 .... **143**
    STEPH DAVIS
    'EXPECT THE UNEXPECTED'

CHAPTER 15 .... **151**
    REBECCA WILLIAMS
    'PRACTICE MINDFULNESS'

AFTERWORD **159**
    APPLYING THE METHODS OF EXTREME ATHLETES IN NOT-SO-EXTREME SITUATIONS

REFERENCES **170**
PHOTO CREDITS **178**
ABOUT THE AUTHOR **180**

INTRODUCTION

Being afraid happens to all of us. Everyone experiences fear at certain times in their lives. It may be during a raging snowstorm at base camp in a mountain range, or during a meeting at work where you think for several minutes about voicing your opinion about a new project, but feel paralyzed by insecurity. Wherever and whenever it is, the same rule always applies: if you don't learn to manage the fear, the fear will manage you. Then fear will decide what you do – or dare not do.

If there is one group of people that has gained experience with fear management, then it must be extreme athletes: professionals in sports where you don't necessarily run a serious risk of getting injured, unless things go wrong and then the chances of injury or even death are relatively high. For this book I have interviewed 12 of the world's most successful extreme athletes, as well as 3 of the best sports coaches in this discipline.

The extreme athletes consciously take that risk a couple of times a week – or even once a day. They climb buildings or rock walls thousands of feet high without a rope to hold them if they slip, or mountain summits 26,000 feet above sea level, often having to deal with frozen body parts or altitude sickness. They balance hundreds of feet in the air on a tightrope with just a thin cord around their waist to break their fall, or jump from fixed objects with a parachute or wingsuit, with no small chance of crashing into the ground (on average, 1 in every 60 BASE jumpers dies every year; 72 per cent of them have seen a fatal or very serious accident involving a fellow BASE jumper).

These extreme athletes are not without fear. In fact, all fifteen interviewees in this book are often scared to death. And that is exactly what fascinates me, and made me want to write a book about it. Why would anyone willingly seek out fear? Part of the fascination comes from my own love of climbing. Several times a week, I climb on a training wall around sixty-five feet high, and a few times a year I climb outside, on real rocks. Although I am safely attached to a rope when I climb and therefore, in theory, nothing serious can happen if I fall, I am nevertheless often afraid of the drop below me, and more than once I have asked myself: why do I willingly keep doing this?

Fear is certainly not a pleasant experience. When we experience fear or other forms of stress, our sympathetic nervous system almost immediately triggers a 'fight or flight' response, which readies our bodies for action. Our blood pressure and heart rate increase; blood is taken from our organs and sent to our muscles to increase their tension. Our pupils dilate, our hearing becomes sharper, our digestion slows down and saliva is produced less quickly, so our mouths become dry. At the same time, we begin to create moisture in other parts of our body – sweat ensures the body can cool down after explosive action. If the stress persists, the pituitary gland in our brain instructs our adrenal gland to produce cortisol, adrenaline and other stress hormones. These cause the blood sugar level to increase and the metabolism to work more quickly again, so we can generate more energy to take action. And that is what makes our knees knock and our other limbs shake violently.

For a long time, researchers have believed that extreme athletes are sensation-seekers and abnormally fearless. That they are constantly looking for a thrill in their lives, because they naturally have less dopamine in their bodies than other people and constantly need external adrenaline kicks. Without these kicks, it is argued, they would drive themselves to despair through boredom.

Another well-known explanation is that extreme athletes under-assess their own vulnerability, and therefore completely underestimate the risks they take. But in recent years, researchers have had increasing doubts about these kinds of theories. The assumptions about pathological adrenaline junkies appear to be based on wafer-thin evidence, often relying on poorly conducted research on very small or unrepresentative samples. Furthermore, newer research produces completely different results.

A team of researchers that investigated the motivation of extreme athletes to climb rocks or jump from high places concluded, for example, that they are very much the opposite of reckless and naive. They are very realistic about the risks they take, and mindful about safety (or the lack of it) in their sport. That they nevertheless take risks has nothing to do with a naively positive outlook, but is because they have faith in their own sporting abilities. And this faith, the researchers assert on the basis of their observations and interviews, is also realistic. The athletes who participated in the study were not only passionate about their sport, but also knew many useful rescue and other safety techniques.

This picture of a thoughtful and skilled athlete also better matches the personal accounts of famous mountain climbers that have been written down for posterity. Take, for example, alpinist Heinrich Harrer, who in 1938 became the first person to climb the north face of the Eiger. Harrer wrote 'Without doubt, people are small and insignificant in nature. [...] Even the ridiculous earthworms know that icicles can be blown off. But they have learned to closely observe when and where that happens and they attempt to avoid the danger.'

In other words, mountain climbing is dangerous, but it helps if you know about your environment and you take steps to avoid as many risks as possible, according to the circumstances.

Or consider the reflections of Joe Simpson on his journey in Tibet, which he describes in his book 'Storms of Silence': 'The sheer scale of these, the world's highest mountains, was breath-taking and humbling. They induced in me a delight and a passion I could scarcely believe I possessed, and at the same time they would intimidate and humiliate me and quash any vain hopes I had of climbing them. There was a precarious balance between confident ambition and fearful insecurity about venturing up these soaring peaks.'

I don't hear in Simpson's words the voice of a fearless stress addict but of someone who wants to do something yet is, at the same time, afraid of it. He doubts whether he should do it – but does it nevertheless, because the desire to overcome the fear is stronger than the fear itself.

Moreover, other research shows that, for most extreme athletes, the 'thrill' is really not so important. They have various motives of much greater importance, such as the feeling of freedom that many of them experience while engaging in their outdoor activities, the pleasure that they get from being active and in the natural environment, the personal growth that they undergo by developing new skills, and the increasing self-confidence that they derive from overcoming their fears and extending their boundaries.

If we manage to overcome our fears, what follows, according to Stephan Enter in his novel 'Grip!', is 'the overwhelming sensation of freedom and happiness, where your feet and hands do not climb the mountain but where you feel like you carry the rock and the sky and the pure air with you when you climb. It is a trance; you're embracing oblivion but at the same time seem to be alive more than ever, with all your senses experiencing joy. Because it is so joyful to be corporeal, to have a body and to feel – every touch, even every pain; what a joy to be able to tense your muscles and with clenched energy smoothly climb higher, meter by meter'. [translated from the Dutch by author]

The difference between extreme athletes such as Harrer and Simpson or those interviewed in this book, and most other people in the world, is therefore not the absence of fear but the skill they have developed to overcome it. Extreme athletes don't engage in their sports because of fear, but *despite* it. Alain Robert (chapter 1), for example, does not let his fear of heights stop him from climbing buildings, and Steph Davis (chapter 14) is afraid of falling but is still brave enough to jump from high rocks in a wingsuit. They are able to overcome the mental barrier, because they have learned to recognize and control their fear. I argue that we should replace the label 'adrenaline junkies' for 'fear experts' if we want to describe them.

Each of the extreme athletes that I have interviewed has developed their own effective method to perform well despite their fear, and they talk about this openly in this book. Their lessons are not only applicable to other extreme athletes, but to everyone who experiences fear at certain moments in their life. People with stage fright, fear of speaking in public or breaking down in front of big groups. People who dare not drive a car, or who would like to change their career, but are too frightened to let go of their comfortable lives.

Luckily there are a number of ways to overcome fear and self-doubt once and for all. The very best of these are described in the following fifteen chapters.

CHAPTER 1

ALAIN ROBERT

'BE PASSIONATELY DISCIPLINED'

GETTING FRENCH CLIMBER of buildings Alain Robert on the telephone long enough to talk to him about fear is no easy task. For a start, it's hard even to get him on the phone at all.

It's not that he doesn't want to be interviewed. On the contrary. Robert – who is nicknamed 'Spiderman' because he climbs skyscrapers without safety gear (and also, by the way, without asking for permission from the authorities to do so) – was among the first extreme athletes who agreed to talk to me for this book.

He likes to talk about his ascents, especially because he has suffered from vertigo his whole life and has learned from his own experience how you can overcome deep-rooted fears.

But wanting to talk is one thing; being able to is another. Despite his vertigo and the fact that, according to his doctors, 66 per cent of his body is handicapped because of earlier climbing accidents, Robert constantly seems to be at high locations where it is impossible to interview him.

MONTPARNASSE

The first time I call him on his cell phone, Robert is inside the 722-feet high Montparnasse Tower in Paris. He is walking around on the ground floor, inspecting the tower from the inside out, to prepare for the

Chapter 1 - Alain Robert

climb that he wants to do later that same week. 'I can't call right now', he whispers to me. 'I'm trying to find out how strict the security is here, and I have to be fast, before the security people start wondering what I'm doing here. Call me later this week.'

The second time I call him, a few days later, proves to be even worse timing: Robert is no longer on the ground floor, nor is he inside the building. He is about to climb the Montparnasse tower. He started a day earlier than he had planned, because it had been an exceptionally quiet morning, with hardly any security officers walking around the tower. Robert decided he couldn't miss this opportunity. 'So it's not a good time to be interviewed', he apologizes. 'The tower has fifty-eight floors, so I'll be climbing for a while. And the connection is not too good either. Call me back tomorrow!'

Third time lucky. 'Spiderman' now has plenty of time to talk about his climbs and his strategies for overcoming vertigo, because he is in his car, driving back to his house in the French countryside (after this book was published, he moved house to South-East Asia).

'For the next few hours, I'll be close to the ground,' he says. 'That's an exception in my life.'

BAD PREPARATION

His ascent of the Montparnasse Tower was successful, Robert tells me, but it wasn't an easy climb for him. 'I reached the top in about forty-five minutes, but I experienced a lot of challenges during the climb. That was mainly because I hadn't prepared so well. Ideally, I prefer to test climb a building a bit before I start the real thing. I usually do that during the night, so that nobody can see me. I get to know the structure of the building and can decide which climbing shoes will work best on it: for example, I'll select tight ones with a lot of grip on the soles when the building feels slippery, or more comfortable shoes when it has plenty edges for me to stand on. The main advantage of a test climb is that it gives me some idea of what to expect. Secondly, it increases my confidence. After I've climbed the first few feet of a building, I know for sure that I can do it. Knowing that makes the ascent more enjoyable.'

But this time he could not test climb the building. It is strictly forbidden to climb the Montparnasse Tower, and it is closely guarded day and night. As soon as he saw that there were few security people around, he decided to go. Perhaps he shouldn't have done that. Because of that spontaneous decision, Robert started the ascent without information that is crucial for a builderer.

For the first ten feet or so, he had to move fast to get beyond reach of the security people. Robert knew that they generally don't dare to follow him up high so, after he'd reached the first floor, he could slow down. Unfortunately, by then, he had realized that he was wearing the wrong shoes for this type of building. To climb the Montparnasse Tower, he would have to push the noses of his shoes as deeply as possible into the slits around the windows. But the insteps of the shoes he was wearing were not high enough for that and they wouldn't stick. With his feet slipping off, he was forced to use extra arm-muscle strength to avoid falling down. Climbing in that way cost him a lot of energy. He was sweating, he felt exhausted... and yet he still had many floors to go.

CEMETERY

He sighs deeply. 'To be honest, it was a very scary and dangerous climb. Usually when I come home after an ascent and my girlfriend or my son ask me how things went, I can tell them that I had fun. But that wouldn't be a fair answer this time. Yes, once I had reached the roof of the building and was safe – then it was fun. But until then, was a struggle. Halfway up the tower, there was a moment where I literally had to fight for my life. I don't often consider the fact that I might die during a climb, but this time I did. My foot slipped and I pulled myself up with my arms. I looked to the right and there, next to the tower, I saw a cemetery. "Well", I thought, "at least I'm taking the shortest route to that place".'

He laughs, but when he starts talking again, his tone is more serious. 'See, even though I'm an experienced climber, I get scared. I knew all the way up that a feeling of fear was disturbing my concentration, and I felt that my arms were pumped. So I tried to find resting positions as often as I could and I tried to shake the tension out of my arms, but even then....I felt strange, not comfortable, not safe.'

At such scary, life-threatening moments there is only one solution, says Robert: grit your teeth and push on. In his eyes, that is the only way to overcome fear: putting yourself in a situation that is so stressful that there is no time or space in your mind for self-pity or doubt.

'Giving up is not exactly an option', he says drily, 'because you'll die.'

Hearing him talk like that makes you wonder why he voluntarily puts himself in such dangerous situations, but Robert claims that he has no option. The attraction of the height is stronger than his fear, and he is able to push through that fear 'with a lot of passion and willpower.'

SELF-DISCIPLINE

Psychologists would call that skill 'self-discipline', or the ability to control your impulses, emotions, desires and behavior. People with a lot of self-discipline choose long-term rewards (I will reach the top and be proud of myself) over short-term ones (if I stop climbing now, I don't have to feel afraid anymore). Social scientists regard self-discipline as one of the major predictors of success: research has shown that high-performing university students usually score very high on self-discipline. That factor is even more important than having a high IQ in achieving goals and being successful.

It is very likely that Robert would do well on a self-discipline test. 'You have to understand that I don't climb skyscrapers because I am suicidal,' he says. 'Dying is the last thing I want! All I want is to climb.

One problem is that it is dangerous; another is that I am very aware of the risk I am taking while climbing. So, in order to survive, I have to be able to deal with my fears and doubts.'

Robert believes that being afraid of heights is normal for climbers. 'It's a physical response to height that most people experience. You feel dizzy, you want to go down, you feel scared...In that respect, climbers are just like people who stay closer to the ground in their daily life – we all get afraid when we are in high places. But the difference between us and non-climbers is that we have learned how to stop that fear from turning into overwhelming panic. Because you simply cannot afford to panic once you're high up on a rock or a building. That would make you hyperventilate, and lose concentration and muscle-power. And yes, then you have a fair chance of dying. If, on the other hand, you feel some fear but are able to remain calm, you will still be able to reach the top safely. I prove that every time I stand on the roof of a skyscraper, celebrating my success. But I had to learn to control my deep fears before I was able to do that.'

Indeed, self-discipline is not a natural-born trait, but something you can develop and improve. Psychologists have found that there are various things you can do to become more self-disciplined: for example, selecting attainable goals (because unrealistically high goals are demotivating), or choosing one goal rather than many different ones (this will increase your chances of success, and that is motivating). The third and most important step involves practicing your self-discipline frequently – daily, if possible – for example, by forcing yourself to do things that you don't feel like doing, such as washing up, not eating that delicious-looking desert, or taking an ice-cold shower in the morning. Studies have shown that these methods can even increase self-discipline among people who typically find it hard to resist temptation.

That being said, it is true that certain character traits, like having a strong will, will have a positive effect on the development of self-discipline. That Robert has a strong will becomes clear when he talks about the time when he started climbing, in his late teens. He used to live in the French Ardeche region with his parents, and they would often find him staring at the rock faces near their home. The young Alain imagined that someday he would stand on the tops of those rocks, only he had no clue how he could make that dream come true.

Nevertheless, after he had seen a picture of professional climbers in a magazine, he decided that that was what he wanted to be, a climber. Two minor challenges lay ahead him: he had never climbed in his life, and he suffered from severe vertigo. Yet the mountains called. Robert started to hike up to them, after school and mostly all by himself. Moving slowly and extremely cautiously, he started to climb on relatively low pieces of rock. Without a rope, because he simply didn't have one. And every time, he was scared to death.

DIZZY

'I'd sit down on the top of a not-so-high rock and force myself to stay put there, looking down at the ground. In that way I tried to get used to the height. At first, I would tremble and get dizzy, and I was convinced I would fall off.'

But the more he practiced, the better he became at keeping calm despite his persistent fear and dizziness. By the time he was seventeen, Robert was climbing every day and noticed that he had become quite good at keeping his vertigo manageable – even at impressive heights. After finishing high school, Robert found a part-time job for eighteen hours per week – the rest of his time he spent on climbing.

He started to take his friends to the rocks and came to realize that he not only enjoyed climbing, but also had a talent for it. Moreover, he clearly had more self-discipline than others of his age.

'Many of my friends were afraid of heights, just like I was. But I was able to suppress that fear with my mental strength, and they weren't. I could get to the top of each route, even if I felt scared, while they often gave up halfway. I never allowed myself to give up. I always stayed focused on the long-term goal: becoming a professional climber. When they wanted to go home, I begged them to do one more route.'

So the difference between Robert's climbing friends and himself was not that he had a better technique, or that he was stronger. The difference was that, for his friends, climbing was just a hobby – something they did for fun. For Robert, climbing was much more than a hobby. It was a deep love. He felt he was cut out for a climbing life. And so climbing didn't have to be fun; he just had to do it. 'Overcoming fears is not fun', says Robert. 'It's hard. You'll only do it for things that you want so deeply, that you cannot imagine life without it.'

Most psychologists and mental coaches would probably agree with Robert. Developing self-discipline is much easier when the goal that you want to reach is very valuable to you. That is why most people find it easier to set money aside for that trip around the world they've always wanted to make than for a debt they have to repay. Similarly, smokers who try to quit because they consider the habit a threat to their health will likely have more success than smokers who try to quit because their partner is constantly complaining about their bad breath. Self-discipline is all about motivation.

Because Robert was highly motivated, it was not hard for him to find the self-discipline he needed to practice daily to overcome his vertigo. And before he knew it, his dream to become a professional climber had come true. 'I was discovered by sponsors and started making money by climbing. The sponsors asked me whether I would consider to try and climb a building. They said it would draw attention to my skills, as it was something hardly anybody was doing back then. I agreed immediately. I just wanted to climb, I didn't care whether it was on a rock face or a building.'

BETWEEN LIFE AND DEATH

Robert has since climbed the Eiffel Tower, the Grand Arche, and the Montparnasse Tower in Paris. He has also climbed the Empire State Building in New York, the Golden Gate Bridge in San Francisco, the Taipei 101 building in Taipei, the Burj Khalifa in Dubai, the Sydney Tower and the Opera House in Sydney, and both the Petronas Twin Towers in Kuala Lumpur. Just to name a few.

'When I climb I feel completely free. Most of the time I enjoy climbing, I feel blessed to be able to do it. Sometimes I am afraid. It's part of the deal for me. And that's okay, because it is that fear, and my own ability to master it time and time again, that makes me feel so strong after an ascent. I know I can control the fear. I know I can force myself to keep climbing, even if my body is giving me signals that it would prefer to give up and escape the fear. The feeling I get when I have reached a top of a skyscraper....I can't even describe it.

Every time I climb, I exist in a place between life and death for a few hours. It is as though I have to win back life during that time. And if I reach the top, I feel like a winner. I have never felt more alive than in the hours after a successful climb. All of my senses are sharp, and I feel intense gratefulness for being alive, for having my loved ones in my life, for everything that I like or find beautiful.'

He is willing to train hard for that feeling, both mentally and physically. To keep his body strong, Robert works out daily in his home, by walking over his ceiling like a spider. He has fixed holds to the ceiling and has taught himself to hang on to them for at least twenty minutes. After his daily spider-walk, Robert exercises in more simple ways in and around the house: push-ups, pull-ups, 'planking' – a fitness exercise where you bring your body into a completely horizontal position to train your stomach muscles. Most people do a planking exercise with their hands and feet on the ground, only lifting their hips and chest. On his Facebook account, a photo shows that 53-year old Robert does the exercise in the air, hanging onto the metal bar of a giant hoist crane.

Sometimes, he doesn't feel like working out, he admits. But he does it anyhow. 'Working out can be boring,' he says. 'But at least it serves a higher goal. I mean, it's not like...washing the dishes, or something like that. That is just as boring, but it doesn't bring me anything good in the long-term either. I don't care about a clean kitchen. I care about climbing.'

Even more important than his physical training is his mental training. Robert still makes sure he frequently practices being up high. If he didn't, his vertigo would become stronger again. And so he climbs and he climbs, even if he is ill or very busy. Once more, he emphasises that self-discipline is not hard to find when it comes to climbing. 'Willpower is no problem as long as you are truly passionate about something. It comes naturally.'

That is the main lesson that he wants to teach people who have a dream for the future, like he used to have. 'Especially people who have a dream, but don't dare to try turn it into reality because they doubt whether they are able to do all the things needed to achieve it. To work hard and do things they might be afraid of. To those people I would like to say: if you are completely honest with yourself, you will know whether this dream springs from your deepest passion. Is it something you want to do for yourself, or because it gives you status, or because your parents or your wife want it for you? In the latter cases, you'd better give it up now. If it had been my parents who wanted me to become a climber, I would never have found the self-discipline to fight my fears. But if you truly want something, you will be able to get there.'

ACCIDENTS

The combined power of wanting something badly and having a strong will proved to be enormous after the many accidents that Robert experienced. When he was nineteen years old, he fell from fifty feet high and broke both his wrists, the bones in his heels, and his nose. He underwent three operations and started climbing again. Within a few months, he was climbing at his old level.

A little over ten years later, he fell again. This time from a height of eighty-five feet. His head and hands hit the ground. His wrists were shattered. Robert was in a coma for several days and had to recover in hospital for two months. Doctors told him that he would never be able to climb again, but they had underestimated Robert's willpower.

'I listened to what the doctor was telling me. And then I listened to my body. And my body told me that I was in a lot of pain, and that I would have to go through a lot in order to climb again, but that it was possible. So, once I was back home, I started to set myself climbing goals. I wanted to progress little by little, each day a little more. And eventually, I wanted to be able to climb again.'

Not far from his house, there was a brick wall. It wasn't high, but it was long. Robert would walk up to that wall and try to traverse from end to end. He stayed low to the ground, and would mark the place on the wall where he fell off. The first few times he tried it, he could not move at all. His fingers wouldn't hold onto the bricks, his legs were heavy and weak. But he gained his strength. After a few days he was able to move his hand sideways, then his body. After that he fell to the ground. He placed a mark and came back the next day. And the next. And the next. Eventually, he was able to traverse the wall. And two years later, he was climbing better than ever.

And he is not planning to stop climbing any time soon.

'My dream is to climb the tower of an oil company in France when I turn sixty. That age is a symbolic one to me. It is the age where people start to perceive you as 'old'. And I want to show myself and the world that at that age, I will still be strong enough to do what I like best in life. With that goal in mind, I continue to train my body and mind.'

But what if the day comes on which he will be too old to climb, I ask? Robert is silent for a long time before he finally answers me. 'I don't know. Climbing is what I do – it has been like that for so long. If that passion were taken away from me, I'd no longer exist.'

CHAPTER 2

ALEX HONNOLD

'FEAR IS A REACTION TO THE PAST. DON'T LET IT DETERMINE THE FUTURE.'

ALEX HONNOLD (1985) IS PROBABLY THE MOST FAMOUS CLIMBER IN THE WORLD. HE CLIMBS ROCK WALLS THAT ARE THOUSANDS OF FEET HIGH, AND HE USUALLY DOES IT WITHOUT BEING FIXED TO A ROPE, AND WITHOUT USING OTHER GEAR THAT COULD RESCUE HIM IN CASE ANYTHING GOES WRONG.

During climbing, Alex just wears special climbing shoes with lots of grip on the soles and toes, a chalk bag with climbing chalk so that his hands can get a good grip on the rock, and during long climbs, a rucksack or bum bag with some food and drink. Apart from that he just uses his bare hands. This type of climbing is known as free-solo climbing, which is seen as a branch of the sport that has a relatively high risk. One slip at a great height and a climber will fall to their death.

BOY-NEXT-DOOR

Thanks to the risks that Honnold takes, he has become a star in the US. He appears regularly in the newspapers, features in adverts, and his book 'Alone on the Wall' (2015) that talks about his climbing exploits flew high in the bestsellers' list for many weeks. In June 2017, Honnold was all over the news when he completed the first free-solo climb of El Capitan in Yosemite National Park in California. The 31-year-old climbed the nearly 3,000-foot wall in three hours and fifty-six minutes – without ropes or any protective gear.

The accomplishment required unparalleled physical skill as well as a singular mental focus, and it was received with shock and awe by the audience. Journalists and writers came up with all sorts of clarifications why and how Honnold is able to keep calm under extremely stressful circumstances and, while most of his fellow professional climbers congratulated Honnold with his amazing achievement, some of them also questioned publicly whether the risk he had taken had been too big. Perhaps Tommy Coldwell, one of his close friends and fellow climbers, summed the ambivalent responses up best in a personal and eloquent article called 'Why Alex Honnold's Free Solo of El Cap Scared Me': 'We all know Alex is the greatest climber of our generation. I trust him with my life. I trust him a little less with his own.'

By now, Honnold might well have grown tired with the world's fascination for his apparent fearlessness. In 2016, Jane Joseph, a neuroscientist and professor at the Medical University of South Carolina, even investigated his brain to see what makes it possible for him to stay focused and precise in dangerous situations. Joseph put Honnold in an functional magnetic resonance imaging (fMRI) scanner to see how his brain responded to fear stimuli. The climber also filled out a survey that psychologists use to assess so-called high-sensation seekers, people who pursue thrilling or dangerous experiences. It was found that Honnold's brain showed very little amygdala activity to stimuli that most people would have a stress reaction to, such as disturbing or scary photos.

That lower-than-average reaction could be what drives Honnold to seek out more extreme experiences. However, that conclusion is weakened considerably by two main factors. First of all, the same research showed that other aspects of Honnold's behavior didn't fit with traditional sensation-seeking patterns. Typical sensation-seekers are impulsive and lack conscientiousness, the behavior trait that helps people regulate their actions. That makes them prone to risky situations, as well as vulnerable to substance-abuse problems. Honnold's has little in common with them. The research suggested he is extremely conscientious. Moreover, Honnold does not drink, smoke or use drugs.

Secondly, it remained unclear from the research whether Honnolds' ability to stay calm should be considered a fixed trait – an unusual functioning of the brain – or whether it is a skill that he has developed and learned, by consistent exposure to scary situations. That latter scenario seems the most probable, considering the fact that Honnold has experienced fear many times in his life. He is not fearless. He just knows how to perform well, despite of fear.

That Honnold does get scared is shown, for example, by the fact that he decided to bail out when he first attempted to free solo El Cap in November 2016 because it 'didn't feel right' after few hundred feet up (he descended a series of fixed ropes to the ground). It is also shown in the video footage in 'A Fearless Climber', a film made in 2010 about Honnold's climbing life.

In the film clip, Honnold (then 23 years old) can be seen climbing the Half Dome, a wall over 900 feet tall in Yosemite National Park, and getting into a state of panic.

He stops climbing, and instead shuffles to one side to a narrow ledge (with the suitable name 'Thank God Ledge'), spreading his arms out horizontally against the cliff to keep his balance. 'I'm freaking out,' he says to the filmmakers. After that, he stays on the ledge for some seconds in silence, looking at the enormous emptiness in front and under him. He's a man with a boyish appearance, big dark eyes, and noticeably skinny legs that stick out from his shorts. The viewers can see that he pushes himself against the rock, appears to hyperventilate, but forces himself to relax, and then calmly completes the climb.

The film clip does not remind you of a person with a dysfunctioning amygdala. Instead, it demonstrates that the key to learning to manage fear is the combination of intense physical training, perfecting techniques, and applying the psychological technique of mental rehearsal. Honnold has followed exactly these steps, through hundreds – if not thousands – of hours of climbing.

In our interview, he emphasizes that rehearsed training is crucial to performing optimally in stressful situations.

'I've typically had a mental list of routes I'd like to solo some day and then worked towards them in a roundabout way. The physical preparation is really straightforward. I just climb a lot and make sure that I can easily climb the style and difficulty level required to free-solo the specific route. In principle I don't use ropes or other gear when climbing, but you must realize that I only do routes that I'm completely sure that I can climb on my own, without too much difficulty.'

'So before I begin a free-solo climb, I practice the route a number of times with safety gear. I climb with a rope as many times as I need, until I no longer threaten to fall, until I no longer make mistakes, and I feel totally safe and self-assured at every moment of the climb. By practicing with a rope I can make the movements that are necessary to do the route, without a mistake being fatal. If I lose my footing somewhere then I fall a maximum of ten feet or so, and the rope catches me. You don't see that in most film clips about me, but this is how thoroughly I prepare.'

This narrative shows something important about Honnold's fear-management techniques: he does not just train his body under normal, non-stressful circumstances. Instead, he often trains his physique under mildly stressful situations (with a rope, but high above the ground and with the risk of a non-fatal fall), until he feels ready to get the job done under very stressful situations (without a rope). Psychological research suggests that this strategy may be key to success. Nevertheless, it is not yet commonly used by sports coaches or in other professions dealing with high-risk.

For example, police officers usually train their shooting skills in fake, unrealistic situations (they shoot at plastic images of persons, that don't move) which might explain why they often miss the target in real-life shooting incidents, even if they perform extremely well in training. Shooting with a high heartbeat and a fear of death, demands different skills than shooting in a safe training-environment. Research projects in which police offers practice their shooting skills in simulations of robberies and other stressful events, showed that these officers perform much better during real high-risk situations, than officers who only practiced their skills in non-stressful circumstances. Likewise, visual simulation programs have significantly decreased the amount of air accidents caused by pilots. These examples show that training the skills needed for extreme sports or other high-risk activities, are most effective if they are executed in situations that are (mildly) stressful.

Honnold also has to feel fully prepared psychologically before he goes up a rock face without a rope.

'It is complicated to describe how I mentally prepare for free-solo climbs, because the technique I use changes every time. I guess the main thing I do is think a lot about the route I would like to do. Visualize every aspect of it, how it will feel as I do it, how it would feel to fall off, how it will feel to get to the top. Sometimes I spend a lot of time preparing and still don't feel ready mentally. Basically, if a route seems scary than I don't do it. Fear, to me at least, is a sign of unreadiness.'

But the opposite can happen, too: 'Sometimes inspiration just strikes, even if I haven't rehearsed a route or prepared at all. For instance, this happens on routes where, based on my climbing experience, I'm totally sure I'm fit and technically good enough to climb it.'

And yet fear can sometimes strike during climbing, such as when Honnold was on the Half Dome in his early twenties and was overwhelmed with panic, or more recently, when things 'didn't feel right' on El Cap and he decided to lower off halfway a free-solo. Fear never completely disappears, he says, but he is getting better and better at managing it.

'Doing climbing, I've had many things happen that have given me a massive jolt of adrenaline and I've had to calm myself down again – a hold breaking while soloing, let's say. You can quickly learn to ignore what your body is doing at such moments and carry on like normal. You've got no other option.' Because being in a state of fear while climbing can be dangerous: it impacts the way in which you move, and makes it harder to think clear. And as such, it increases the likelihood of falling.

SHOCK

As an example, Honnold talks about the time that a big piece of rock that he was holding during a free-solo climb came loose. 'If something like that happens, your body is almost in a state of shock for a little while. Your heart pounds, your legs tremble or ache, crazy things like that. But I have learned: none of these things need to have any bearing at all on the climb ahead of you. They are a physiological reaction to something that already occurred. They basically don't matter at all for your performance ahead. So you can learn to ignore them entirely and carry on like normal. Which calms you back down a lot more rapidly. So, if I get very scared because a piece of rock comes away from the wall and so my hold is gone, or I lose my footing, I know that doesn't mean anything about the rest of my climb.'

When I ask him how he learns to get calm quickly after such an intense physical reaction of panic, he humbly says that he has no magic trick, other than just practicing a lot. 'I think it's a practiced skill, and most people just have very little practice. It is an understanding that I've gained through years and years of climbing: fear is a physiological reaction to something that happened in the (recent) past. Your hand can suddenly not be holding onto anything, or your feet come away from the rock, and you think: "I'm gonna fall!". And in that order: first something happens, and then you get scared. And the fear can get so big that it takes you hostage, and impacts on everything else you do. But you losing your footing does not make any difference to the rest of the challenge. You can just grab another piece of rock, and put your foot comfortably on another ledge. So then you keep climbing, and reach the top.'

According to Honnold, you can teach yourself to nip small bursts of fear in the bud straightaway, by deliberately relaxing yourself and not letting the rest of your climb suffer. 'I feel like I've gotten good at recognizing the signs of fear in my own climbing. If I realize that I am doing those things during a climb, a rational part of my mind steps back - as if I am looking at my own behavior - and I say to myself: "you're scared; you need to relax".'

Then he does his best to take deep, slow breaths, tries to relax his grip and does something he describes as 'softening my focus. That means that I look around more, but less focused. It's a bit like looking around less intensely: I see more, and can take in more. It's all very straightforward, but obviously it's easier said than done if you're scared and have to do it!'

So this is what Honnold's technique comes down to: instead of going along with the story in your head at a fearful moment that things will now 'definitely go wrong', that you're scared and don't want to be in that situation, stay true to the facts. It *nearly* went wrong, but from now on it won't. You still have every chance of success. And so you keep going, as if nothing's happened. 'If you do that, you calm down more quickly than when you stay with your fear, or when you believe that a little mistake reduces your chances of reaching the top.'

PLAYING WITH DEATH

Again, Honnold suggests that it is his frequent experience in stressful situations, that has taught him to deal with fear much better than most people. While nobody would dispute that he is extremely good at keeping his head cool in dangerous circumstances, there are many voices who predict that such skills will not prevent Honnold from ultimately falling to his death.

'People often think that I play with death,' says Honnold in response to this criticism, 'or that I don't realize that I run the risk of dying during a climb. But I don't want to die and I also don't believe that there is a big chance of me dying while climbing. I make sure I only do climbs that are so easy for me that the chance of a fall is tiny.'

'That is not to say that I block out the random risks associated with free-solo climbing. Of course, my foot can slip. Or a stone can fall on my head, which means I'll let go of the rock and fall. I feel like it's important to understand and acknowledge the risks, the same way that I don't block out the thought of dying in a car accident. There is a real, albeit very small, chance of dying every time I drive on the interstate. I accept that each time I get behind the wheel. Soloing is the same. With every climb I accept the risk that I could fall and die or do myself serious harm. I accept that risk in my sport, because I believe it's realistic but small. It's the price I have to pay to be able to live this way.'

So Honnold does not deny the risk, and in this sense agrees with the people who predict that his climbing career could cost him his life. But at the same time he underlines that he knows what he is doing, and that his risk assessments are realistic.

EL CAPITAN

And yet, it is not only people who don't know about climbing who are concerned about the risks Honnold takes. In a climbing magazine, a fellow climber described Honnold's methods as quite irresponsible.

The writer, who climbed El Capitan, the granite mountain wall in Yosemite National Park, with Honnold, stated that though the latter did not climb without a rope, he only attached himself onto a few points in the wall, and so risked falling tens of feet. Were this to happen Honnold maybe wouldn't die, but he could nevertheless seriously injure himself if he smacked hard into the rock.

Alex Honnold says he knows the article and is on good terms with the writer. But he doesn't agree with the conclusion. 'The quote about risking huge falls doesn't quite give an accurate sense of what went on on El Cap. I might have gone 98 feet without placing gear, in theory risking a fall of let's say 229 feet, but that's on a terrain of my choosing, where the climbing is far under my level. If at any moment I get scared I can always place a piece of gear and make myself safe again. Being comfortable with long runouts just comes from a confidence in that level of climbing. It's definitely not true that I'm never scared of falling when I'm climbing, and so take big risks. What is true is that I know I won't fall off of easy cracks.'

Therefore, though Honnold sees the danger in what he does, he thinks differently to most people about the point where the risk becomes unacceptably big. Put simply, he gets scared later than others do. And he admits that the point at which this happens has moved over the years. As far as heights and climbing are concerned, his fear threshold is many times greater than most others.

FLAT PAVEMENT

Honnold's fellow climber and good friend Hazel Findlay – also interviewed for this book – explains it to me thus: 'In his climbing Alex feels just as safe as when another person walks on a flat pavement or a sloping dune. It is possible to stumble, also in these instances, but relatively speaking there's a small chance that that will happen. How scared of that are you? Not at all, right? You simply go for a walk without feeling frightened, though no-one could deny that in principle it's possible to fall. That is the same for Alex, except that he climbs what we see as complicated and dangerous.'

Many of Honnold's free-solo climbs are, according to the generally accepted classification system, easier than what he could climb given his talent and experience. And yet – as with the kerbs and dunes – the risk of serious injury remains. Though Honnold does climbs that are easy for him, they are still high walls, and he would be very unlikely to survive a fall. Staying calm in these situations could suggest over confidence or an under estimation of danger, but according to Alex that is not the case. He says that he remains calm in objectively dangerous situations thanks to his ability to handle his fear – and this ability seems to have grown out of practice under mild stress.

'I have definitely improved at managing my fear over the years, so I think that's very much a learned trait. I think by being in scary situations fairly frequently I've learned how to deal with them a lot better than most people. Yet even for me, the level of fear rises and falls on a day-to-day basis. I get scared leading sometimes, even when I'm totally safe and there's no real reason to be afraid. But I've also learned to appreciate when that's happening and do my best to overcome fear. Calming myself is not something I was born with! It is a learned skill. Overall, your comfort zone only increases over time. As you have more and more experiences that stretch your comfort zone it eventually becomes quite large.'

'If you have more experience doing things that you find scary, fewer situations will frighten you. I'm now comfortable with all kinds of things in climbing that five or ten years ago would have seemed totally crazy.'

'My experience with fear of dying also means that I don't worry about minor setbacks. Whenever I meet people who are super anxious about things in normal life, like stressing about missing a flight, taking the wrong train or buying the wrong product in a store, I always think that they need more mortal peril in their lives. They need some actual, real danger in their lives to put everything else into perspective. If they know how to handle justifiable fear, it will automatically become easier to deal with stress caused by something relatively unimportant. Staying alive is the most fundamental thing to worry about. Everything else is sort of a distraction.'

CHAPTER 3

ALEXANDER SCHULZ

'LET GO OF EVERYTHING THAT YOU DO NOT NEED'

Perhaps the best way to describe Alexander Schulz (26) is as an equilibrist with a taste for great heights. The young German is specialized in a sport that very few people dare to do: walking along a very narrow 'slackline' about 1-inch-wide, suspended high up in the air. And high means high: around 460 feet above the ground. In 2014, Schulz broke the world record for highlining (slacklining at great heights) by walking at that height along a slackline 1,230 feet long.

BETWEEN HEAVEN AND EARTH

While he balances on the slackline, Schulz is attached to it by an elastic strap. One end is fixed to a harness around his waist and the other to the line. The strap makes sure that, if he lost his balance, he would not fall to the ground, but would end up dangling in the air about 5 feet below the slackline.

Still not a particularly relaxing position for most people, but Schulz has become used to being somewhere in between heaven and earth with no ground below his feet. He talks about his experiences modestly and calmly, seemingly unimpressed by his own achievements. Though what he does may seem bizarre to outsiders, Schulz emphasizes that his balancing acts are seen as less of a big deal within the world of slacklining. 'It's not something I can live from. The competition for sponsors is high.

Chapter 3 - Alexander Schulz

I am lucky enough to be able to live with my parents and having them to support me financially every now and then, otherwise I could not have done this professionally.'

As a child, he had never imagined himself becoming a professional highliner. Schulz suffered from severe fear of heights when he was younger. He was born and raised near the mountains, and whenever he joined his parents for a hike and came close to an edge of a drop, he would grasp the ground with his hands and crawl way forward until he had reached a safer, less exposed spot. The space around him would always make him dizzy and afraid, he now recalls with a sense of amazement in his voice. It seems hard for him to reimagine the fear he must have felt back then. But apparently a fear of heights can be unlearnt. Nowadays, when he hikes over mountain slopes, he sometimes feels concerned about slipping and falling. But he no longer feels afraid of the height itself.

'I am not afraid when I am balancing on my highline, either. At least, not any more. I used to be. But I have learned, by practicing a lot, that nothing can happen to me. I am attached to a strap, so even if I stumble, I will not fall to my death. Highlining seems much more dangerous than it actually is. As soon as a highliner has learned not to be afraid of the height, and of the space around him, he can start to experience the great joy that is inherent to the sport. Being surrounded by nothing but air and nature gives you an indescribable feeling of freedom. When you are highlining, you are moving in a void – you are so high up there that you hardly hear any sound, and there is literally nothing to hold on to. You are a small dot in the universe.'

But the first few times he tried to walk on a highline, Schulz was not yet able to enjoy that sense of freedom. He was too afraid. 'I found it hard to trust the elastic strap and the harness. They had to save my life if I fell. What if the strap snapped, and I plummeted to the ground? I was so scared I didn't dare to fall. Even worse, I hardly dared to move! I took mini-steps, and every time I thought I was about to lose my balance, I would bend my knees and sit down on the line, so that the harness would not have to catch my fall.'

He tried to be braver, but every time he felt he was losing control while walking on the line, he would do the same thing. 'As soon as I wobbled a bit, I would almost automatically squat down and grab the highline with my hands. I just couldn't stop myself.'

SWAYING LINES

But he didn't give up.

He set up a slackline closer to the ground and started practicing falling from there. Only a few feet above the ground, he would let himself fall and practiced not grabbing the line, but keeping his hands close to his body so that the harness would catch him. By doing this exercise for weeks and weeks, tens of times a day, he eventually learned to trust his safety gear. Just as he had eventually overcome his fear of heights as a child, by hiking through the mountains year after year.

Nowadays Schulz feels confident enough to move freely on the highline, and is no longer afraid to lose his balance. As paradoxical as it may sound – it is precisely that lack of control that makes him a better slackliner. He explains that, in order to keep his balance, it is much more important for a slackliner to control his mind than to control his body.

'People who see me walking on a highline mostly believe that I have perfect control of my body. And to some extent that is true, but it is not that simple. A slackliner's body needs to be both relaxed and tensed. Say that a slackline is 100 feet long. That means that the wind will make it sway in the air. Moreover, by walking over it, *you* will make it sway! If the line moves in a certain direction, your body has to move along with it, otherwise you will lose your balance. If your body remains as stiff as a board while the line sways to the left or the right, you will undoubtedly fall. But if your body is less rigid and follows the line, you will be able to keep your balance. So, yes, you do need to be able to control your body to be a highliner. But part of that control is the ability to consciously relax your muscles, to make your movements flow, almost.'

That contrasts sharply to the hard focus of the brain, which is required to concentrate on the task ahead. 'As a slackliner, you have to be able to remain calm at all times. Your mind can only be filled with thoughts and feelings that can help you to perform at your very best. You cannot let yourself be distracted by negative thoughts, or, even worse, to lose faith in yourself because of doubt and fear. At the very moment you allow yourself to consider the possibility of falling, you are increasing the chances of that happening.'

I CAN DO THIS

That is what almost happened to Schulz while he was attempting to break the world record in China. All seemed to be going well, until he was halfway along the slackline. Suddenly the wind started blowing, very hard. Immediately, the slackline started swaying wildly through the air. Schulz moved along as best as he could, from left to right, and back. At such unexpected, stressful moments, your mind is typically inclined to think the worst. 'A very negative thought flashed into my mind', he recalls. 'Something like: "Oh no, with this wind, I'll definitely lose my balance!". And immediately after I had thought that, my body stiffened up.' He felt his muscles tense up, which was exactly what he didn't need at that moment, with the wind all around him and the line swaying back and forth below his feet.

Just in time he was able to regain control of his mind.

He suddenly remembered a time when he had been slacklining in similar weather conditions. The wind had been blowing like it was now, but he had not fallen off the line. That memory proved to Schulz that he still had a chance to break the world record. 'Suddenly I was convinced that I could do it. And I started to repeat, in my mind: "I can do this. I've done it before. I can do it again. I can do this".'

He didn't lie to himself. Every time he repeated those positive thoughts in his mind, he felt his body relaxing more and more deeply. He could feel his muscles becoming less tense again, and that he was regaining control over his movements. 'I controlled my mind, and my mind controlled my body.'

LET GO OF WHAT YOU DON'T NEED

Schulz has learned to control his mind in stressful circumstances through a technique that he describes as 'letting go of everything that you don't need.' He believes that this method is not just useful for extreme sports like highlining, but also for other challenging situations where you need to remain focused.

'Whenever you find yourself faced with a challenge, like I am whenever I have to walk along my line, then let go of everything that will not help you to reach your goal. Only take with you what will help you to perform at your best.'

For slacklining, this means that Schulz tries to avoid certain thoughts and emotions. He has made a deal with himself: if he notices that he is getting angry at himself, for example when a training session is not going well, he consciously puts that feeling to one side. He does the same with frustration and insecurity. These are all frames of mind that he doesn't take with him on the line. He will not allow himself any feelings of doubt when he is steps out on to the line or to get angry if he loses his balance for the fifth time in a row. 'There can be no space for such mindsets in my head. Nor do I want to be concerned with distracting thoughts when I am slacklining, like "there are people watching me, so now I have to succeed!" As soon as such a thought pops up in my mind, I set it aside. Thinking such things won't help me succeed. They will only make me doubt myself, and make it harder to enjoy my sports. It is much more useful to focus my attention on a mindset that will help me in my performance. Being calm. Self-assured. Concentrated. Those are the only thoughts I allow into my mind when I'm slacklining.'

It is not easy to forbid yourself to think or feel certain things, Schulz admits. But he has a solution to that: instead of trying not to think or feel something, you should fill your mind completely with frames of mind that are will help you during your challenge. 'You can only think so many thoughts at one time, right? So, if you concentrate on positive thoughts, there will be less space in your mind for the negative ones. I help myself to concentrate on positive stuff by talking to myself in an encouraging way: "I can do this", I say quietly to myself while balancing. "I'm doing just fine. I feel super-calm. I'm enjoying it".'

STAYING CONCENTRATED

Besides repeating positive affirmations and setting aside unuseful thoughts or emotions, Schulz uses another technique that helps him improve his sport performance: training himself to stay concentrated.

To be able to cross a highline without losing balance, Schulz not only has to focus intensely, he also has to keep that intense focus going for a long time. Depending on the length of the slackline, it can take up to one and a half hours to cross it. If Schulz did not train himself to maintain an intense focus for a long time, his mind would probably get distracted before he was even halfway along the line. And if that happens, there is more room for negative thoughts to enter his mind. 'The first half is usually doable for me. I am focused and determined. But around halfway or so, sometimes my mind gets tired. Suddenly I notice that the other end of the line seems so far away... Before I know it, I am doubting whether I will make it. That is a sign my concentration is fading.'

To prolong the time span of his concentration, Schulz regularly practices focusing intensely for longer periods of time in non-stressful situations. He will attach the ends of a slackline to two trees in a park nearby his house, and then start walking it along it. He goes back and forth for an hour, sometimes two... He focuses consciously on his feet, the soft swaying of the slackline, his breath, or the music he hears through his earplugs. At those moments of intense, continuous concentration, he feels as if he is moving through a tunnel, where all he can see is the line and his own body – the surroundings seem to have disappeared. The advantage of this regular practice in the park is that it prepares him to keep the same focus in situations that are much more stressful – like when he is trying to break a world record.

In China, he noticed very clearly that his concentration practice had worked. After he was briefly distracted by the wind and the one negative thought that was triggered by it, it was relatively easy for him to refocus his attention onto his feet, the line, and the music he was listening to through his earplugs. He crossed the second half of the line in an optimally positive mood, he recalls, 'and with the most intense hyperfocus I have ever experienced in my life so far.' Positive thought after positive thought filled his mind. He smiles when he thinks back to that hour on the line: 'I felt absolutely confident that I would reach the other side. And when I had, indeed, managed to do that, it dawned on me what an enormous power our mind has'. Your thoughts are a force of energy – a force that can make you win, or lose.

Schulz' powers of thought must have grown extraordinarily fast, because – although nobody would probably expect this from a world record holder – he only started highlining five years ago. He thinks that he has been able to become one of the best in his sport precisely because he started off being afraid of heights. It forced him to think about fear, and how that was impacting his performance. 'After the first few attempts – the times when I could not stop myself from sitting down on the line as soon as I was afraid of falling – I started to ask myself questions. "What is it that is making me so afraid? How does my body feel when I get scared? And what helps me to calm down? How can I calm myself when I am on the line? What would I need for that?".'

These were complex questions that he had never tried to answer before in his life. But his new ambition forced him to do so. He would ask himself these questions every time he practiced highlining. Slowly he started to get to know himself better. He learned what typically frightens him (having to trust his safety gear), what makes him nervous (a lot of people watching him) and, most of all, he learned how to calm himself in stressful situations.

MENTAL POWERS

Schulz is convinced that these lessons have not only helped him succeed in his sport, but also in other areas of his life.

'Reflecting on fear has taught me how much we can accomplish by using our mental powers. I am not talking here about anything mystical; all I mean to say is that, if you find yourself in a challenging situation, it helps to talk to yourself in an encouraging way. Likewise, you can ruin things for yourself by thinking or talking negatively to yourself – I believe a lot of our failures in life are the result of negative thoughts or convictions.'

If you think you have no chance of getting your dream job, you are unlikely to even try and send off that application. Or, if you do, you might get invited for an interview and go there without any hope or self-confidence. That mindset will most probably negatively affect your chance of getting the job. To improve your mindset, you could think back to other jobs that you applied for successfully. Or you could make a list of compliments you have received from former colleagues. Or sit down and write a list of all the tasks you have completely successfully at work. These exercises help to fill your mind with positive thoughts and feelings, and eventually, to convince your future boss that you are the person for the job.

'If you want to be happier in life, or if you are dreaming of a completely different life than the one you are leading now, it is important to realize that you are able to accomplish a lot more than you might now be aware of, if you learn to understand and guide yourself. So make a serious goal of your wish, think about what you need to do to accomplish that goal, and think about what you should let go of to remain focused. That requires a lot of practice, but it's worth it: it might just get you to the other side of the line.'

CHAPTER 4

ARNO ILGNER

'BECOME AWARE OF YOUR 'NOW-MOTIVATION' AND FOCUS ON THE LEARNING PROCESS'

Arno Ilgner is an American-born rock climber and a pioneer in the field of mental training for climbing. In the 1970s and '80s he became known as a brave climber, someone who dared to test his skills on rock faces that others thought intimidating. As he got older, he developed an experience-based mental training method, known as The Warrior's Way, that became very popular in the climbing world.

Ilgner's method involves a step-by-step programme for improving performance and overcoming fear and insecurity. The popularity of his method becomes clear from his packed yearly schedule. A date for an interview with Ilgner has to be planned many months ahead. It's not that he doesn't want to talk to me any sooner, he tells me in a short phone call, but the problem is that he truly doesn't have any spare time at that moment. Not even at the weekends? I venture to ask. No, he's busy giving clinics. What about the evenings? No, he has to write blogs and keep his website up-to-date. Well, isn't he planning for any holidays in the near future? Ilgner is quiet for a few seconds, then sighs. Nothing on the horizon.

The waiting turns out to be worth it. When we finally have our interview, Ilgner patiently explains his vision to me. He thinks through each question thoroughly before answering it. If he speaks, he does so with a language that is full of management jargon. He talks about 'challenges' when I ask him about bad performance; and he consistently speaks of 'learning opportunities' when I try to get his take on failing.

Ilgner warns me early in our conversation that he prefers not to talk to me about fear – even though he is well aware that that is the topic of this book. In his view, that would be taking things one step ahead of where we are. Before we can discuss fear, we need to talk about what factors underlie it. Ilgner believes that it is mostly not fear itself that hinders people in reaching their goals. Instead, there are two other problems that make it hard for them to perform at their best. The first is a lack of understanding in the motivation for change; the second is mis-focused attention. Both problems can result in self-doubt, frustration and, indeed, fear.

Ilgner explains that if people long to reach a certain goal but find that they don't seem to get anywhere near it, they might *think* that it is the fear that is holding them back, while actually they will have to solve these two problems before they can work on anything else. And they can do so by constructing an analysis of their motivations to reach their goal, and by increasing their mental focus on the learning process that will help them to eventually reach it.

UNDERSTANDING YOUR OWN MOTIVATIONS

On the first problem – the lack of understanding about our motivations to want something – Ilgner says, 'Roughly speaking, there are two types of motivations that can serve as a driver for goals. The first, I like to call the 'end-motivation'. It is related to the end result – your future dream. It can be material things that you would like to have or do at some day, like having that nice house or that dream job, or it might be the goal to be able to perform in sport at a certain level.

The second type of motivation I call the 'now-motivation', and it relates to things that are happening at this very moment of your life, like a boring day at the office, or climbing training that did not go well. Those are things we typically don't like in our lives. We want to get rid of them – and that is why you develop the goal of having a different, more successful life. Most people aren't completely aware of their now-motivation. They know precisely what they want to reach in the future, but they aren't very clear on what aspect of their present lives, they would like to see changed. To put it very simply: what's wrong with what you have or do, now? You need to be able to answer that question in order to reach your future goals.'

Ilgner claims that most people are focused on abstract goals that exist in the future. We might want to become a professional climber, one day, or we fantasize about quitting that boring office job and becoming a musician. There's nothing wrong with having such dreams, he says, but they will not help you to turn them into reality. 'End-motivations enable us to dream about our deepest hopes and expectations in life. As such, they offer us important insights about who we are and what we want, but they do not offer us any concrete steps or tools to turn our dreams into reality. For that, we need to understand our now-motivations.'

That last sentence is important, says Ilgner, and he repeats it – just in case I missed a word or two. It means that, as long as we allow ourselves to daydream about our goals, we do not provide ourselves with realistic chances to actually reach them. 'This is what happens frequently,' he says. 'Say you are an amateur climber, and you want to become very good at climbing. That is your goal, and with that goal you turn to me for help. The first questions I will ask you will be related not to your future dream, but to the present: "What are your weak points in your climbing career now? What is the first intermediary goal that can help you to measure your progress, such as a certain mountain that you want to climb, or a regional competition you could join in?".'

Ilgner would work in exactly the same way if he met a person with a very different type of goal, for example, the office worker who wants to be a musician. He would ask them what is bothering them about the work in the office, and what would be the first financial precautions they would need to take in order to be able to quit the job. 'Knowing your end-motivations will not help you to answer those questions,' he says.

End-motivations are weak tools for action because they show merely what we want, and not so much *what we do not want any longer*. 'And that is so important!', exclaims Ilgner. 'Why do you want to become a good climber? Is it because you expect that learning new techniques will fulfil you with joy, or is it because the climbers around you are better than you and you feel you need to compete with them? And what makes you want to quit your job at the office? Is it because you don't like that type of job or your present working environment, or do you miss creativity in your life, and are you hoping to get more of that if you become a professional musician?'

Knowing what you want in life is clearly not enough – to reach the goals you aim for, you will need to understand why you developed that goal in the first place, and once you know that, you will have to define the steps you need to take to get from your present situation to the reality you dream of.

MISFOCUSED ATTENTION

According to Ilgner's theory, there is yet another problem that hampers us in reaching our goals: the misfocused attention with which we tend to approach those goals. Because people generally focus their attention on the end-result, we forget to pay attention to the learning or transformation process that we have to go through to eventually reach that goal. That lack of focused attention typically results in confusion, stress or frustration – and that will negatively impact our chances of success.

In an article in a climbing magazine, Ilgner was once quoted as saying 'Anxiety and the fear of failing originate in focusing your attention too far ahead, on the unknown future. It happens to all of us. Be aware of it when it happens, and guide your attention back to the present.'

He explains these words during our interview by giving an example.

'Imagine a female rock climber, who dreams of becoming the best in her sport. Then imagine this climber has selected a goal that can help her measure her progress – she wants to climb an iconic rock face. Now, here she is, standing below that rock face, strongly determined to reach the top. She will focus her attention to the highest point of that wall, and is already thinking about the moment that she will be done climbing, celebrating her success on the top. I argue that there is a fair chance that, halfway up the climb, she will become dispirited by the long distance that still lies ahead of her. As a consequence, she will become overwhelmed with self-doubt about her strength or technique. That will turn into outright fear; she will start breathing faster and more superficially, her arm muscles will get pumped due to the tension in her body and the lack of oxygen, and she might have to give up her attempt.'

That is what Ilgner considers a double-missed opportunity: 'Not only has she not reached her goal because she misfocused her attention, she has also failed to see this climb as an opportunity to develop her climbing skills. While that was her end goal, right? To become a better climber!'

By focusing all of her attention to the top of the rock face, the climber might have missed the pieces of rock right in front of her. She might not have noticed what mistakes she made, or what things went well in her climbing. She wasn't aware what it was precisely that made her scared or dispirited. 'And because she has not gathered all this valuable information about her own performance, she is unable to grow in her sport. The next climb will present her with precisely these same problems – she will not have learnt to deal with her weaknesses.'

It would have been much better if the climber had avoided looking at the top of the rock face, instead focusing her attention on the pieces of rock closer by. 'Don't look too far ahead. Don't think "Oh, that goal is so far away, I am not sure whether I can make it that far." Instead, concentrate on the very first move you have to make with your hand or foot. Notice how fast your heart is beating. Can you calm yourself by breathing deeply through your mouth? Are there body parts that you could relax more? Then make the next move.'

At the moment the climber started to feel overwhelmed, rather than trying to move closer towards that goal and ignore that feeling of self-doubt, Ilgner would have advised her to pause and reflect on questions about the factors underlying it. "What makes this particular project so challenging for me? Are there any weaknesses that I would need to work on in order to be able to climb the route with greater ease? Could I already start addressing any of those weaknesses here, on this wall?".'

Such questions aren't easy to answer for people who find themselves in a scary or otherwise uncomfortable situation, I politely object. Ilgner agrees immediately: 'No, they aren't. But I never promised a short-cut to success. I believe that fears, doubts and not reaching our goals offer us opportunities to develop ourselves. Those experiences can get you to a better place than you are in now. But that happens only if you use them strategically, and that means you should not go through them and then forget them as soon as you can, but rather the opposite: you have to re-live them, reflect on them, investigate them until you understand what happened to you at that frustrating moment.'

To make sure you do so, it is wise to begin each attempt with that one central question in Ilgner's work: what is your now-motivation? Once you're clear on that, the whole experience of 'failing' will feel like a learning experience. 'If this climber's true goal is to become the best in her sport, then this particular climb might feel to her like a success, if it taught her some new techniques and mental insights that she will need in her climbing career. But if she feels she failed, well, maybe then she should investigate her motivations again. Because to me that says that her goal was not to improve, but to climb this rock face perfectly at first attempt.'

CLIMBERS AND NON-CLIMBERS

Although Ilgner originally developed The Warrior's Way for climbers, he has become convinced over the years that it is also helpful in other life situations.

'My method can help us to gain insights into our own goals and expectations. It helps you to understand how your motivation to reach a specific goal is linked to fear and self-doubt, and it teaches you how to overcome those emotions so that you can perform at your best. Those lessons are not just useful for ambitious climbers, but also for people who feel unhappy with their present career. The Warrior's Way can support them in re-evaluating their life and propelling it in a new direction.'

It may seem a large leap: from career doubt to a panic attack that a climber gets halfway up a high rock face, but Ilgner claims the difference is not as big as it seems. 'You could imagine both situations as a footpath, on which you stand. You want to get from here to a different place – a place where you believe it is better, more beautiful. Whether you are a climber or an office worker, and whether you want to reach a mountain top or a career-planning goal, it will always be crucial to stop focusing your attention on the end-goal and concentrate instead on the task at hand. Start by investigating your now-motivation, and then focus on the actions that you need to take *now* in order to reach your goal later.'

For the office worker, this means that he should stop daydreaming about the exciting life of a pop musician, filled with fans and concerts. 'That is typically what people do who are unhappy with their lives; for hours and hours, they fantasize about some radical life-changer that will make everything right – but I know from experience that this is not what they truly need to become happy.'

Ilgner explains that people often think they are unhappy because of their job, while in reality it is a relatively small problem within that job that is bothering them. 'If that is the case, then a career shift will not make them happier. In the case of the office worker, it is not the work that he dislikes – it is just the fact that he misses creativity in his job. Perhaps he used to play in a band when he was still a student and gave it up after he'd started his career, and now he is starting to feel unhappy because he misses making music. He blames his job for his unhappiness, but a career switch will not necessarily bring creativity back into his life. Not even if he succeeded and turned his dream of becoming a musician into reality. Do you know how many musicians make a living by playing the same cover songs at weddings and other festive events? There's nothing very creative about that...'

Ilgner laughs: 'If this guy really is looking for a positive change in his life, he'd better reflect on those now-motivations. Or he might end up in a pretty miserable situation!'

DAYDREAMING

But say the office worker has done some thinking and concluded that it really is his job that is making him unhappy, and is confident that being a musician would make him happier. Then he is ready to take step two of Ilgner's method: subdividing the end-goal into intermediate goals, and focusing his attention on those intermediate goals – one by one. This will help to prevent him from being overwhelmed by a far-off end-result, and offer insights into the concrete steps that need to be taken to eventually play in that band. 'Maybe he can start taking music classes, or join an amateur band in his free time. He can try and arrange gigs, or record a single and send that out to radio stations. If things go well, he can consider spending less time at his office job and more in a studio. That way, step by step, he is heading towards his goal – and meanwhile he can reflect on his experiences to learn whether this is indeed what he needs to become happier.'

Not all goals are reached – not even with Ilgner's method. He emphasizes that he does not offer a guarantee for success. Sometimes people define goals that are out of their reach, either because they lack the talent or capacities needed for it (not all of us can be professional climbers or musicians), or because the circumstances in their lives don't allow them to take the steps needed to reach the goal (they may get ill, or lack the financial means).

'It happens quite regularly that people set goals for themselves that are simply impossible for them to reach. Both climbers and non-climbers do that! Therefore, I advise people to see their end goals as potential outcomes of a learning process, rather than as fixed. On their way towards that goal, they might want to pause and take the time to reflect upon their progress and their motivations.'

Climbers can do that by selecting pause points along their route, for example a place halfway up the rock face where they can stand quite comfortably and take a rest. Once they have arrived there, they can consider how the journey has been so far, and to what extent that what they are doing is still matching their end-goal.

But what if the female climber from our examples discovers during such a break that she is simply not talented enough to climb that iconic mountain? Ilgner answers in the stubbornly positive way that is so typical of him: 'Yes, that is very possible. And that only means that she will have to redefine her end-goal. Maybe she should not aim to reach that top, but use this rock face to practice a specific technique. Who knows: maybe, if she is able to develop that technique, she will reach the top of that mountain ten years later!'

For the musician, Ilgner offers similar advice. On the day he quits his office job, he can set a date for himself on which he will reflect on his first months as a professional musician. He might come to realize that his career switch did not offer him the sense of happiness that he hoped it would. No problem, says Ilgner, 'he will just need to redefine his end-goal.'

In both cases, Ilgner insists, the first end-goal was not wrong. 'No at all! The musician and the climber have learned so much by setting those goals for themselves! These experiences will help them to define a new goal, one that suits their character and capacities even better. Reconsidering earlier decisions or changing your mind is not failing, in my view. It is inherent to personal development, it is the only way people can grow. As soon as you start realizing that, life will no longer be about success or failure, nor about fear or courage; it will always be about growth and transformation.'

CHAPTER 5

CATHERINE DESTIVELLE

'GATHER A TEAM OF EXPERTS AROUND YOU'

Catherine Destivelle is internationally recognized and admired as one of the most adventurous female alpine climbers of recent decades. She is still alive and climbing, even if she has come close to dying a few times in her career.

Destivelle prefers to keep her exact age a mystery. What she is prepared to share is that she was born in Algeria, grew up in Paris and started climbing at a young age on the rocks of Fontainebleau – a large forest on the outskirts of the French capital.

She was already able to climb technical routes in her teens, ascending rock faces that defeated other people with relative ease. When she was only seventeen years old, she climbed some of the highest mountains in the alps in France.

WORLD CHAMPION

Destivelle was obviously talented in her sport, but her ambitions reached well beyond climbing. She wanted to study physiotherapy, and so she did. During her student years, she had considerably less time to head to the mountains, but she remained attracted to climbing. Once she had obtained her physiotherapy diploma, she started participating in regional sport climbing competitions. And with great success: Destivelle became world champion, several times in succession. These experiences

Chapter 5 - Catherine Destivelle

made her realize she was extraordinarily good at climbing (or, in her own, modest words, 'I started to understand that I was kind of talented at this sport'), but she also felt that this branch of the sport wasn't her kind of thing. Destivelle longed for the peaks that she had seen as a child when she stared out of the window of her family's holiday home in the French countryside. And even for the peaks that she knew existed beyond them. That longing for the mountains eventually appeared stronger than her professional fascination for human physiology. She gave up physiotherapy and stopped sport climbing, and finally became a mountaineer.

In her mountaineering career, Destivelle's climbs include the classical route on the North Face of the Eiger, the Matterhorn and the Grandes Jorasses.

At some point during our interview, I start to read aloud the long list of mountains that she has climbed, to check that I am not missing any facts – but Destivelle interrupts me with a shy smile on her face, her hand waving in the air, as though she wants to literally wave my words away. 'Yes, yes', she mumbles, 'that should be about right. And it is okay if you forget to mention one or two. By the way, a few of those climbs were not technically complex at all. If I was able to do them, a lot of others could do so, too.'

Her modesty is completely unnecessary, but it typifies Destivelle. A few times during our conversation she will repeat the message that the climbs she has done really weren't that much of a big deal. 'My teenage son thinks it is cool that it made me famous, but for him I am just his mother. He is more interested in his trombone than in my climbing.' And she seems to be content with that.

But if she won't say it, I will: Destivelle's climbs *were* a big deal. Many of them are generally considered extremely tough because she did them during the winter season, and also because she did them all by herself: without a rope team – which would be the usual way to do it.

She reached some of the highest peaks in the world without the support of fellow climbers, and usually also without using safety ropes. Instead, Destivelle preferred to use only her own body to help her ascend, and sometimes, if she felt it was necessary, she would place a safety carabiner along the way.

She has always loved those solo expeditions. She did one in the French Alps that lasted for eleven days; and she did solo expeditions in Africa and Asia. Besides her solo expeditions, she frequently climbed with one or more partners.

LONELY AND DANGEROUS

Not all of her climbs ended successfully. Twice, she had to give up a climb in the Himalaya halfway because of heavy weather. And it wasn't only the weather that often made her expeditions dangerous undertakings: in 1985 she broke her back and pelvic floor after she fell 115 feet down into a crevasse. Nearly ten years later she would make another fall – sixty-five feet, this time – from the top of a mountain in Antarctica, resulting in an open fracture in her shin bone. Injured as she was, she and her climbing partner had to descend for thousands of feet without external support and once they had finally safely arrived at basecamp, Destivelle had to survive for three long days in a simple tent in icy conditions, before help arrived and her fracture could be treated.

Her many lonely and dangerous adventurous attracted the attention of a wide audience – throughout her life, Destivelle has appeared in French newspapers and even played the lead in several climbing movies. By far the most of this attention zoomed in on her solo expeditions. The audience was fascinated by Destivelle's lack of fear. People wanted to know how it felt for her having to fight the elements, all by herself on snowy mountain tops, and constantly endangered by extremely low temperatures or stormy winds. Mountains are unpredictable. What could she do if things took a turn for the worse, journalists would ask her? As she reflects on that question during our interview, her answer is rather sober: 'I could do a lot of things in such a situation, actually. I knew precisely what I was doing. And I don't give up easily.'

But perhaps the most important secret of her success is a technique that she uses, one that does not seem to sit easily with her preference for doing things by herself: this loner claims that she has been able to achieve her highest goals 'due to the people who supported and advised me in my expeditions – sometimes without them even knowing that their expertise was helping me a great deal in my way up.'

Huh? I ask. Destivelle clarifies: yes, it is true that she usually climbed a mountain by herself, but in her mind, she often imagines that a whole team of climbing partners is joining her. 'Only they have no idea about that fantasy of mine!'

'To the outside world, it may seem that solo expeditions are very lonely,' she explains. 'And that image is partly correct. As a solo climber, I set my own goals and I am fully responsible for my safe return. I select the mountain I want to climb, I prepare my own body and mind for the ascent, I pack my own backpack, I decide how much food and gear I need and it is me, only me, that starts hiking. Nobody behind me, nobody to help me make decisions. But that doesn't MEAN that I don't make use of the insights or support that others have offered me during my solo climbs. Before each hard expedition, I made it a habit to approach people who I consider experts and ask them for information. And in my mind, those people and their advice join me during my ascent. Even stronger: without those people, it is likely that I would not have been able to reach as many mountain tops in my life as I have done now.'

STAR PLAYER

This time, her modesty does make sense. Research by American and British scientists on 'star players' in basketball teams has shown that their success is usually not decided by their individual talent, but much more by the support that they get from their fellow team members. Similar findings come from research on extremely successful employees in business environments. Their success is rarely the result of raw talent alone but also builds on the support structure around them. Researcher Mark de Rond therefore concluded that 'your organization may owe you as a star player, but you owe it back for allowing you to be as good as you are.'

For Destivelle, the 'cooperation' with her 'team players' typically starts with her gathering information written or otherwise documented by others. Every year, she selects one or two climbing goals for herself – mountain tops that she wants to reach. She makes that selection on the basis of a couple of criteria. Destivelle prefers certain styles of mountaineering, and that is why she consciously selects climbing routes that are suitable for those styles. She also prefers to select goals that allow her to have a various range of experiences, so she might pick mountain tops in different regions of the world. But most of all, she selects a goal on the basis of the stories of other mountaineers. 'So many climbers have written books about remarkable expeditions! Mostly they talk about extremely challenging routes, or about expeditions that ended dramatically. Some of those stories have turned into classics now. We climbers fear them, and are curious about them.' She got to know many of these stories as a young girl, when she would read books and dream of mountains. All the expeditions she would do in her life were inspired by these or later stories of fellow climbers.

Once she has selected a certain mountain as her next climbing goal, Destivelle will make use of the expertise of her 'team' in a more focused way. She will look for photographs of the mountain taken by other climbers to study its shape, she will read published journals or blog posts about their climbing experiences on the mountain to learn more about common weather conditions or to get to know whether she should anticipate a lot of rockfall on her way. She will read articles in climbing magazines about the attempts of other climbers or, if possible, she might ask them in person about their experiences.

Interestingly, Destivelle often asks these questions without telling the interviewee about her own, concrete climbing plans. Sharing her climbing goal at this phase of her preparation would make her nervous, she says. 'Then other people will start following you, keep an eye on you to see how you are progressing. That would put up too much pressure for me.'

CREATIVITY VERSUS DOMINANCE

That is common among people working in teams. For a long time, researchers assumed that cooperation is more productive than working individually on a project, more recently it was found that there are many instances where this hypothesis is incorrect. In fact, several studies have now found strong evidence that the opposite is true: individuals nearly always score higher on qualitative and quantitative output of their work, than groups. To make things worse: the bigger the group, the lower the achievements. An important reason for these phenomena is that the creativity of introvert-types of people is typically undermined by the dominant presence of more extravert-types of team players.

Destivelle, who might be considered an introvert herself, seems to recognize that dynamic in her climbing experience. As soon as others start to give her advice during her expeditions, she feels pressured to move faster or allows herself be distracted from her own performance. That is why she prefers to make use of her 'team' without actually enlightening its 'members' about her plans.

'From the information I read or hear, I learn about the most difficult passages on a mountain, I get to know where the weather is likely to change fast, and where I should be extra careful about loose rock or other problems. That detailed information helps me to create an action plan for my own expedition. A plan that suits me and my way of climbing.'

With that plan, she starts to look for even more specific information from her 'team'. She might approach people that she knows personally in her immediate climbing network, and ask them for tips and suggestions about the gear that she might need for this particular expedition, such as freeze-dried food, ropes and clothing.

Thinking out loud during our interview, Destivelle admits that she could probably have done her expeditions without hearing more advice from others. She is certainly experienced enough to know what she should take along with her on the road, isn't she? She leaves her own question unanswered for a while, seems lost in thought and is silent for a few seconds. But then the answer sounds determined: 'No. I want to be sure that I am not forgetting anything. In climbing, every mistake can be fatal and so I prefer to always double check with other climbers.'

Again, she does so without telling them about her own concrete climbing goal. 'Then I would lose concentration or feel pressured into starting my expedition sooner than feels exactly right for me. This is why I keep things a bit vague when asking others for advice. I only tell them what they need to know in order to give me relevant advice – but no more than that. And this strategy I would recommend to everyone who is trying to reach a specific goal in life: gather relevant information from people who already know more about your goal than you do, but do not feel forced to tell them exactly what you plan to do. Protect yourself and make sure that you can execute your plan at your own pace and under your own conditions. They are important as advisors, but you eventually decide.'

After she has gathered all the information that she needs and once she feels confident and prepared, Destivelle will start her expedition. At those moments, she no longer feels nervous. Thanks to her research and her team of advisors, she knows exactly what is ahead of her. And even though her 'team players' may not be aware of it, they even help Destivelle achieve her goals along the way.

'They might not know on which day I departed or which peak I want to climb, but of course they suspect that I have a new goal after I have asked them tons of questions. And knowing that they expect me to go on an expedition, gives me strength when I am climbing. Whenever things become difficult, I think of those people. I don't want to quit – if, for no other reason, not to disappoint them! See, climbing itself can be a lonely process, but the support of others can help you to gain the self-confidence and perseverance that you need to reach the top.'

GROUP PRESSURE

Destivelle experienced that positive power of group pressure most clearly when she was climbing a route on the Aiguille du Dru that had never been climbed before. It was 1991, and she anticipated that it would take her eleven days to reach the top. She progressed slowly, and found it very challenging not to lose her motivation, particularly because of the repetitive movements that she had to make to climb this particular mountain. The structure and form of the rock face demanded that she use a hammer and slam pitons in the rock every few feet or so along the route, to which she could attach herself and self-belay her way up. For hours and hours, she had to make the same movements with her arms. It was physically exhausting, and mentally very boring. After sunset she would rest in the wall, the muscles in her arms painful and the sound of the hammer still in her head. 'It felt like it would never end,' Destivelle recalls. 'Every morning I just had to do the same thing. And again. And again.' For the first time in her climbing career, she felt she wanted to quit. The plan to climb the mountain suddenly seemed absurd. But Destivelle managed to push through by thinking of her team of experts.

This time, she had told a couple of the people whose information she had used for her preparation about her plan. 'It was an exception. I had told a little bit about my plan, and only to a few people. I had shared a bit more than I usually did, because I already expected beforehand that this expedition would be very hard for me. Harder than anything I had done before. Knowing that there were people who knew I was on my way, helped me to not give up. It was as if they were cheering me on, looking over my shoulder – even though they were not physically with me. I did not want to disappoint them, so I kept on hammering. I kept on climbing. That group pressure proved a major factor of success in this expedition.'

But she reached the top due to her own strength and efforts, and therefore it is only logical that the route would be called after her. The 'Destivelle route' would be the first climb in the world to be named after a woman. 'Yes, that is true', Destivelle says in a soft voice when I ask her what it meant to her to have a route named after her. 'It's nice, but not that important. There are so many routes in the world, and they all have names. So...what is the next question?'

STUPID MISTAKE

She is clearly much more comfortable when answering questions about expeditions that did not work out well. When we get to talk about the times where she owed not just her success, but even her life, to the help of others, Destivelle speaks with enthusiasm. 'Take the fall that I made during an ascent in 1965. I would not have survived that without the support of my then boyfriend and climbing partner, Erik Decamp. We were climbing in North Antarctica and we were using a rope – something that I did not usually do in my own climbs. So I felt very safe – perhaps a bit too safe.'

She made a 'stupid mistake' when she and Decamp arrived at the top. 'We were taking photos of each other on the top. I stepped backwards without looking where I was planting my feet, lost my balance, and fell over the cliff. I shouted to Erik "Get the rope!" He grabbed it, very quickly, but I had still already fallen 65 feet before the rope stopped me. So there I was, hanging onto that rope with an open fracture in my leg. I remember looking at my wounded leg and realizing that Erik had saved me, but also knowing that there was a fair chance that I would still die.

Chapter 5 - Catherine Destivelle

Antarctica is not a good place to get seriously injured. We were days away from the next town, and we didn't have a helicopter to get us down from the mountain. We didn't even have a phone or a walkie-talkie. It was just the two of us. The situation was very serious, and the longer I was hanging on that rope, the more convinced I became that I would not make it. How was I supposed to descend with a broken leg?'

Her climbing partner proposed trying to descend together. He would build a belay point, use that to lower Destivelle down with the rope, climb down himself, and then repeat the procedure. She agreed – of course, as she had no other choice if she wanted to live.

It took them sixteen hours to get down. Destivelle still has clear memories of how afraid she was during all those hours. Not only was she in severe pain due to her broken leg, she also noticed that the toes of her other foot were starting to freeze. Hanging in the rope, she constantly tried to wiggle her half-frozen toes, while trying to ignore the pain in her other leg.

After they had arrived at the base camp, at the foot of the mountain, DeCamp left Destivelle behind in a tent, while he went to look for help. It was minus 31 degrees Fahrenheit and Destivelle was cold and scared. She tried to keep herself calm by breathing very slowly while he was away – a technique she remembered from her physiotherapy studies. It helped a little, but she did not feel any new hope until she saw DeCamp's silhouette appearing on the horizon, three hours after he had left her. There he was! With a sledge. And he even had some food and a walkie-talkie with him. Destivelle started to believe that she might survive the expedition after all.

But things got grim again. Their radio calls remained unanswered and the weather conditions were so bad that it was impossible to use the sledge. It would be three more days before their calls were finally picked up by a rescue team, and a helicopter was sent in to rescue the couple.

It is ironic, says Destivelle, that she felt much more lonely during that expedition with DeCamp than during any of her later solo climbs. 'In the hours after the accident, I was completely turned inwards. I think I needed to do that to stay calm and fight against the pain. In that sense, Erik could not help me. Only my own mental power could save me. And Erik was also turned inwards emotionally. He felt responsible and was thinking of plans to save us. So it wasn't like we were talking about what was happening to us a lot, or that it was a truly shared experience. Each in our own way, we had to get through that horrible situation.'

Perhaps that is what climbing has taught her first and foremost: how to reach goals by making use of the expertise of others, but especially, by trusting only yourself. 'In the end, it is you and you only that is responsible for the decisions you make,' she says seriously. Then she laughs. 'So just make sure you never make the stupid mistakes that I made that time.'

CHAPTER 6

CEDRIC DUMONT

'DEVELOP A STATE OF HYPER-AWARENESS'

JOURNALISTS HAVE DESCRIBED Belgian BASE jumper and stuntman Cedric Dumont (1972) as the 'man who is able to fly'. And rightfully so: with the help of a parachute or wingsuit, Dumont is able to fly through air for hours. It is a regular practice for him: he has made over 10,000 jumps from airplanes and jumped an additional 2,000 times from buildings, rocks, windmills and bridges.

To do that safely, you need not only a broad repertoire of physical skills, but also mental tools. And Dumont has them. He likes to talk about the strategies he uses for successful BASE jumping: in his blog, or directly with the athletes that he coaches. Or with me, for this interview. He is enthusiastic about my idea to write a book about fear, he tells me, because being afraid of something and doing it anyway – well, that pretty much sums up his way of life. And he loves to share the knowledge that he has gained on these themes over the years with others.

HYPER-AWARENESS

The main method he uses to BASE jump safely entails developing a state of flow, or, as Dumont calls it, a state of hyper-awareness. When you find yourself in that state, there are no thoughts about mistakes you may have made in the past or about what might go wrong in the future. What remains, is pure concentration on what you need to do right now, at this very moment. According to Dumont, everyone is in principle capable of learning how to develop this state.

'Of course, to BASE jump successfully you have to prepare physically, you need to have technical knowledge, to understand how the wind blows and how to use your gear, but more important than all that is to reach a state of hyper-awareness. When I reach that state, I become so completely focused on the task ahead, that everything around me disappears. Because I am no longer distracted, I act precisely and take the correct decisions. You could define this state as an optimal state of consciousness, where we feel at our best and are able to perform to our limits.'

That definition resembles the one coined by the Hungarian-American psychologist Mihaly Csikszentmihalyi for his concept of 'flow': being completely engaged in an activity that is related to the accomplishment of a personal goal. In his work on flow, Csikszentmihalyi explains that, while the human mind tends to be chaotic – full with thoughts and associations that follow one another quickly and without logical order –

it becomes concentrated during a state of flow. This allows us to perform at our best.

'Exactly!', Dumont says. 'People think I possess some kind of magical secret that allows me to jump so often without falling to my death, but the truth is much less mystical. Every time I jump, I am hyper-aware. That is the one and only trick I have taught myself in my BASE jumping career. I had to: in my profession, it's either flow or die.'

BRAIN DEFECT

People who are not familiar with Dumont or the sport of BASE jumping sometimes think that he must be crazy to do it. One journalist accused him of having a brain defect, Dumont recalls. Others claim that he was born without fear, and that he needs the sport to get a kick out of life. But Dumont emphasizes that he doesn't owe his success to a lack of vertigo, or an overload of bravery. He is, in fact, quite often afraid when he thinks about the jumps that he will make in the future. And he doesn't like that feeling: 'It comes with the sport, but I don't like being afraid. So that's not why I BASE jump.'

What attracts him to the sport is not the fear itself, but the need to control those fears. And over the years, he has discovered that for him, the best way to do so is to develop that state of hyper-awareness. 'I do that during each and every jump, yes. Without it, I would fail, because it would mean that I would be distracted and unfocused. When I am flying in between buildings, I don't have much time to think about my next moves. If I reacted too slowly to, say, a change in the direction of the wind, I would crash into a wall or window. So it is of crucial importance that I focus all my concentration on the present moment when I am flying.'

Dumont calls the time that he spends in the air the 'perfect moment to practice living in the now'. These are the moments in his life where he is most aware of himself and his immediate environment, without being influenced by others, or by his own thoughts and concerns. 'And I mostly have a lot of thoughts in my head and tasks on my to-do list,' he chuckles. 'I have a young son, a coaching business – plenty to think about.'

An additional advantage of his method is that the state of hyper-awareness allows him to enjoy the flight more intensely. Although he can feel anxious before taking off, he experiences relatively little fear during the flight, because his mind is completely occupied with the things that he sees and feels along the way: the building from which he takes off, the air, his body, his suit. There's really no space left in his mind for fear. But Dumont is certain that as soon as he lost focus, the fear would start to creep up on him. And that might result in his first unsuccessful flight ever. To avoid that, Dumont constantly focuses his attention on the little things that he has to do during a jump: measuring the wind direction, checking the pressure, making a curve.

MENTAL COACH

Dumont knows it for a fact: hyper-awareness is a requisite for success. 'And that is not only the case for extreme athletes like me! It is true for everyone who needs to perform in stressful situations. Especially people who need to do that a lot: entrepreneurs and managers, for example, or athletes.'

Dumont communicates this message all the time to the athletes he coaches. They admire him for his coolness, his calm appearance under high pressure. He insists that he is no different than they are: it is the hyper-awareness that makes him so successful.

'I train professional soccer players,' he says. 'Often I hear them saying things like "after missing that pass, I was so frustrated, and I kept thinking why I had made that mistake!" To me, this shows that those guys are going over that one mistake long after they had made it. Which means that they are not concentrated on the game! That explains why the rest of the game, they under-perform. And these are Champions League soccer players, can you imagine? They have loads of talent, they are being paid well, and yet they seem oblivious when it comes to the mental sides of performing. So those guys can really improve if they learn how to develop a state of hyper-awareness.'

Dumont also coaches golfers, among whom he observes the same problem. 'I believe that the difference between a good golfer and the best golfer of the world has to do with the capacity to stay in the present moment. What happens after a golfer has missed a hole? Does he keep thinking back to that mistake? Then there is a fair chance he will miss the next hole as well! And what happens before the game? Is he nervously thinking about the game, already trying to think ahead? Or is he able to focus all his concentration on what he needs to do right now, at this second, at this particular hole? The latter guy will most likely win that game.'

Dumont certainly resembles that last type of athlete, the focused one. He has become so fluent in this skill of hyper-awareness, that he is able to stay in that state most of the day. Not just whenever he flies or jumps, but even when he is having a phone conversation, or coaching a client.

He acknowledges that the need to stay in the present is less crucial for a soccer player or a golfer. Unlike a BASE jumper, they will not fall to their death if they allow themselves to get distracted. Nevertheless, Dumont advises them to practice this method. He even claims that sports coaches should offer special training to their athletes to help them develop a state of hyper-awareness. 'They won't save lives with these lessons, but they will obtain the best ever performances from their athletes.'

The same applies to entrepreneurs, CEOs and other leaders in businesses. 'If they are fully occupied with thoughts about the future of their company, they will not be concentrated on their tasks for the day and, as a result, they will underperform. This will also happen if they are constantly distracted during their working day by thoughts about something that went wrong the previous week. That is such a shame! They would perform much more successfully if they could focus on the present.'

PRODUCTIVE STATE

Dumont tells me about a research project that was carried out over a period of ten years by a well-known organizational consultants' company. The study showed that top managers were five times more productive if they worked in a state of flow, compared to periods in their work where they were distracted by thoughts, concerns or dreams for the future. 'Think of that: it means that if you could work in a state of hyper-awareness on Mondays, you would get as much done as your colleagues in a full week!'

It sounds attractive, to be able to switch on that productive, focused state during work or other activities. And Dumont claims that it is possible. 'You can learn it! Everyone can. And you can even practice it in very simple ways. If you are talking to someone, like I am doing with you now, you can check with yourself to see whether you are truly focused on what the other person is saying, or whether you are thinking of something else. If you are distracted, you can bring your attention back to the conversation. Look at the face of the person talking to you, really hear what he or she is saying. That is an easy way to train yourself to pay full attention to whatever you are doing. And you can use the same method during other activities: putting your child to bed, writing an email, or working.'

The more often you try to become completely absorbed in what you are doing, the more easily you will be able to reach a state of hyper-awareness, Dumont says. And eventually it becomes a part of your way of life – just like it has become his way of life. The trick is to create as many flow-practicing moments in your life as possible – until it becomes second nature. Psychologist Mihaly Csikszentmihalyi would agree with Dumont. In his books and articles on flow, he makes the case for living in a high state of concentration, as this will fulfil us most deeply. He therefore advises his readers to develop the habit of being focused on everything they do as though they were concentrating on a work of art – even if it relates to simple and boring household chores like doing the dishes, getting dressed or working in the garden.

Dumont explains that it helps to focus on physical experiences when we try to become hyper-aware. Is there any muscle tension? Is something tingling? When do you start breathing in and when do you stop breathing out? If you pay attention to all of that during some of the activities you do in a day, Dumont says, you will automatically get yourself into a state of hyper-awareness. And there's no need to buy yourself a fancy meditation cushion. 'You can just do it while you're waiting for the bus!' he exclaims. 'Feel your breath, the wind in your hair, your feet in your shoes.'

Another tip from Dumont is don't start to practice in complicated or stressful situations. 'As long as you are not familiar with the technique, it is helpful to practice in surroundings where there is little distraction for your mind. If you want to do it at work, then make sure that you're in an office where it is quiet and where you cannot be disturbed by colleagues all the time. Later, that won't be necessary anymore – you will be concentrated enough and outside noise will not be able to disturb you, but you need quite a lot of practice before you reach that state.'

WHAT-IF

A third tip Dumont offers has to do with what he calls 'what-if' questions. Examples are "What if the recipient is not happy with the email I just wrote to him?", "What if I can never make this flow method work for me?" or "What if I follow my heart and open my own business, and then lose all my money?" Human beings are typically concerned with what-if questions, and these questions have the tendency to hamper our state of hyper-awareness.

'They are useless,' says Dumont. 'They cause stress and concerns, while they are too vague to be answered. You cannot predict the future. It is always possible that things will go wrong, whatever you do. And the more time you spend on considering all those what-if possibilities, the less time you have left to focus on the present moment.'

If you are practicing achieving a hyperawareness-state and you notice that you are distracted by a what-if question, don't try to answer it. Instead, focus your attention on physical experiences – and get back into the present moment. If that doesn't work because you have already become too concerned about something, Dumont recommends pausing the exercise and focusing your attention on an image or idea that is not stressful in any way. Beautiful clouds in the sky, a nice hike through a gorgeous valley – anything will do, as long as it is not connected to the stress that you are experiencing and the performance you have to deliver. 'Once you feel more calm again, you can resume the exercise. You'll find that it goes much better with a calm mind.'

FUTURE

He sighs deeply, and seems uncertain whether he should speak or not, then does so anyway. Sometimes his plea for the state of hyper-awareness is misinterpreted, he tells me. People think it means that they can no longer look ahead, that Dumont is against future planning.

But he is not. For Dumont, 'living in the now' is a method that exists alongside future planning – and both strategies are useful for people who want to achieve success in life. 'Thinking about where you want to be in the future and making plans is very important. I do it frequently, and I recommend that people with ambition do that for themselves as well, whether they be BASE jumpers or leaders. Just don't do it throughout your day. Take an hour or so a day to plan and think ahead. Take some extra time once a month or once a year to dream bigger, to define your wishes for the future. No hyper-concentration, just allow yourself to dream.'

And then turn back to daily reality. 'Use the rest of your days to practice the development of a state of hyper-awareness, and try to be aware and in the present in situations where you have to perform at your best. If you stick to this approach, you have a good chance of reaching your future goals.'

For example, if your future dream is to get a new job, you could use the state of hyper-awareness to write an email to a contact who might be able to help you, clearly describing your ambitions. If you wrote that email while you were still distracted by your future dreams, you might make mistakes or be less clear in your wording. 'See, that proves the importance of the state of hyper-awareness for establishing success in life,' Dumont says. 'It's just as important as thinking ahead. Big future plans are great, but the development of each plan always starts in the present moment.'

CHAPTER 7

DAN GOODWIN

'DARE TO THINK NEGATIVELY'

Dan Goodwin (1955) is an American climber of buildings: a 'builderer'. During his ascents of skyscrapers and other buildings, he doesn't use ropes, carabiners or other safety gear, except for self-made suction cups that he wears around his hands and feet and that stick to the glass. Goodwin's climbs include the Millennium Tower in San Francisco (58 floors, 645 feet), the 432-feet high Telephonica Building in Santiago, Chile, the 633-feet high Nippon TV Tower in Tokyo, the World Trade Center in New York (1,776 feet) and the CN Tower in Toronto (1,748 feet). That last climb got Goodwin's name into the Guinness Book of World Records.

Goodwin's ascents often attract public attention, but not always in a positive sense. He is well known for the many dangerous-looking stunts he performs during a climb: one typical move is to hold onto a building with only one hand, while dangling his other arm and legs in the air. It doesn't seem to frighten him. 'Anything that can go right, will go right!', his website shouts. Visitors can also watch movie clips of Goodwin doing his stunts – dressed in lycra pants and his hair bleached and cropped.

The gymnastic style of climbing that Goodwin has developed has not only earned him approving nicknames like 'SkyscraperMan' and 'SpiderDan', but also triggered a lot of criticism. Many people consider his climbing style reckless and dangerous. Their main criticism is that

Goodwin is generally unable to prepare for his ascents by practicing, since it is forbidden to climb on buildings. They tend to be surrounded by security personnel and cameras, making it impossible for Goodwin to test-climb them. That means there is no way for him to know what to expect before he starts a climb. And because he does not use any safety gear during his climbs, every miscalculation can be fatal. That risk is increased – according to his critical audience – by the stunts he performs during climbs.

FIRE

But Goodwin has a different opinion on that, and arguments to back it up. Most importantly, he says his motivation to climb is not to flirt with death, or to have fun. He climbs with a mission. There were two defining moments in his life that made him decide to climb and live as he is doing now.

The first was when he witnessed a serious fire at the MGM Grand Hotel in Las Vegas, in which eighty-four people lost their lives. Goodwin, who happened to be nearby when the fire started, saw how that firemen were unable to save the people trapped on the high floors. It was, explains

Goodwin with a voice cracking with emotion, 'horrifying' to observe. He submitted a plan to save the hotel guests to the fire department officer in charge of the rescue operation. Goodwin suggested that he should climb the hotel from the outside, fixing up a simple cable system to get the guests out. The officer was not impressed with the idea.

In fact, he threatened to have Goodwin arrested and ordered him to leave the scene of the emergency. Goodwin did so, but was sad and frustrated, sincerely believing that the victims of the fire could have been saved. The next day, Goodwin knocked on the door of a senior fire department officer and told him about his plan. The fire chief, too, was sceptical, and asked Goodwin whether he had ever tried to climb a building. Goodwin replied truthfully that he hadn't: 'At that moment in my life, I had never even considered climbing a building.' The fire chief told him to go and do that first, saying 'After you've climbed a building, you can come back to my office and tell me how to do my job.'

Goodwin did as the man asked. A year later, he climbed the Sears Tower in Chicago. At 1,454 feet and with 110 floors, the skyscraper was at that time the highest building in the world. 'Suddenly the fire brigade was interested in hearing my opinion about their rescue strategies for fires in high buildings,' he says. 'A lot of the advice that I gave them has now been integrated into official safety plans and regulations. That makes me really proud. By climbing buildings, I am able to draw attention to the work that I am undertaking together with the fire service on climbing and safety.'

CAR ACCIDENT

The other defining moment in Goodwin's life that led him to becoming a builderer was a car accident. It happened several months before he climbed the Sears Tower. He had not yet become a professional climber and climbed rocks rather than buildings. He earned a living with an entertainment act in Las Vegas. From the outside, he seemed to be enjoying a showbizz life full of glitter and glamour, but inside he felt deeply unhappy.

One night, after work, Goodwin was hit by a car while crossing the street. Someone had ignored a red light, driving at high speed. He can still remember vividly how he lay there, on the street, and how he felt his spirit leaving his body. 'I was hanging above my body, as it were, and I could see myself, thinking "This is it. Now I will die".'

But he did not die. Instead, he was severely injured, and it would take him weeks before he could even walk.

In the first phase after the accident, he felt sorry for himself. 'I kept asking myself why this had had to happen to me', he says, a little embarrassed at the memory. But little by little, his self-pity faded and Goodwin starting to realize that something magical had happened in his life. He had been given a second chance.

'Before I had the accident,' Goodwin tells me. 'I lived a relatively risk-free life. If I was climbing, I would always opt for the safe routes. In work, I held onto my well-paid job, even though I knew that being an entertainer was not the type of work that could fulfil me in any valuable way. Basically I was living like most people still do, now. Because we are afraid. Afraid to die, afraid to take risks, afraid for the unexpected, the unknown.'

Having survived a serious car accident meant, in the eyes of Goodwin, that he was supposed to live for another while. 'When I realized that my time had apparently not yet come, I thought "If I want to climb a building and prove to the fire brigade that I'm right, I have to do it". In a weird way, ever since the accident, I felt protected.'

Goodwin interpreted his accident as a sign that he was not meant to die yet. He emphasizes several times during our interview that it is that belief that motivates his climbing, not a longing for public attention or adrenaline, as the wider public often assumes.

VISUALIZATION

There is another thing that people have to understand about Goodwin. He does prepare for his climbs – but in his own way. His climbing may look dangerous to bystanders, but Goodwin knows what he is doing. He will only climb when he feels comfortable and safe in a route. Even though he cannot rehearse his climbs, he spends a lot of time and energy on mental preparation. The most effective tool for him in that process is visualization. It has helped him safely to the top, time and time again. This method is so powerful that Goodwin feels convinced that it might help other people to reach their goals, as well.

'Our bodies don't know the difference between actually doing something and imagining that we are doing it. That means that you can practice something that is hard or scary, just by imagining you are doing it. I can't tell you how often you would have to visualize a certain activity in order to perform it successfully, because that may differ from activity to activity, and from person to person. But what I do know, based on my experience, is this: if you visualize yourself doing something often enough, your body will think you have already done it in real life. And so you will be prepared to do it.'

The method that Goodwin uses for his climbing is known in sports psychology as visualization, and is considered an important mental tool that can help people to perform better. In visualization, you imagine an upcoming event or activity in the most realistic way possible. You think not only about what you will do, but you also think of the sounds, smells and other sensory experiences that you would have. You even try to imagine how you would feel while doing it. A good example is the feeling of sheer joy in your chest or gut after you have scored a goal in a soccer game, or the cheers from your teammates and the spectators. Research has shown that during deep visualization, the muscles move and contract as though you were playing soccer in real life. Not quite as intensely as during an actual game, but enough for your brain's memory to save the patterns of muscle activity. Which means that you are able to rehearse, in your mind, what you want to do at some point in real life.

This is the way in which Goodwin uses the visualization method for his climbing. 'I start hanging around the building that I plan to climb, taking a good look at it,' he says. 'Then I visualize my ascent. I do this for hours, sometimes days in a row. My visualizations are so detailed, that it will actually feel as if I have already stood on the rooftop of the building, before I've even left the ground.'

SEARS TOWER

The first time he ever used the visualization method was in 1981, when he was preparing to climb the Sears Tower. He had no other option. It would be the very first time Goodwin would ever climb a building of such height. 'Some months after the car accident, I had begun to plan and practice for this climb. I made myself a pair of suction cups and for six months, I would climb buildings in Las Vegas. They were much lower than the Sears Tower, and also easier to hold on to. The Sears Tower would be more slippery – I knew that even from looking at it. So after half a year of training, I kind of knew which techniques I could use to climb buildings, but I had no idea whether I would be able to climb something as high and complex as the Sears.'

Unfortunately for Goodwin, there was no easy way to find out. The building was way too well secured to be able to practice climbing it. If security guards caught him while doing it, that would ruin his chance of making a real attempt. What if they tightened the security? All Goodwin could do to prepare was look at the building and imagine himself on the side of it. So that's what he did. Every day, again and again, he looked at it. He would sit down on the other side of the street, with his back leaning against another building, and gaze at the Sears. It was a bit like meditation, he recalls, but a very particular form of meditation, one in which he played a mental video of his upcoming ascent over and over again. That unconventional meditation helped him prepare and, eventually, succeed: Goodwin climbed the tower in seven and a half hours.

The movie that Goodwin played in his mind was certainly not fun to watch. 'I visualized every possible scenario of what could happen to me once I got up there, including all the negative ones. At one point, I imagined that I would experience troubles with my suction cups. I imagined how my foot would slip, how my suction cups would lose their hold, how I would fall backwards, my arms ploughing through the air, and the fear of dying that I would feel...'

Goodwin has visualized many horror scenarios ever since that first time. It is remarkable that he typically focuses on everything that can go wrong. He imagines himself making mistakes, or thinks about all the things that might happen and are out of his control: the wind changes, a window breaks... Goodwin sees it all happening in his mind, but instead these images making him afraid, they stimulate him to think about ways to solve such potential problems.

INTENSE NEGATIVE THINKING

It is a common belief that, in order to become successful at something, you have to think positively. Goodwin claims that the opposite is true: we should all think negatively in order to reach our goals. He laughs as he explains: 'There are not many who would agree with me, I know. It's not a popular message I'm bringing here! But I truly believe that it is better for your performance to train yourself to think negatively. If you are engaged in dangerous sports activities, like I am, or if you are about to face another challenge in your life, it would be stupid to deny the risks that come with failure. It would be much better to recognize your risks long beforehand, so that you can make an emergency plan for yourself that will save you if things do indeed go wrong.'

Goodwin believes that the scary vision of the slipping foot and the trouble with his suction cups that he had right before he started climbing the Sears Tower saved his life. 'It gave me an idea for an emergency plan. While visualizing myself falling off the building, I realized that it would be much safer to take with me some sort of hooks, just in case my suction cups would not stick all the way up. And indeed, after I started climbing, I noticed that the suction cups were not suited for the structure of the building. I started slipping! But I didn't panic and was able to act quickly and efficiently, because I had taken the hooks with me. This experience taught me that you have to prepare mentally, completely. And by that I mean to say: don't just daydream about how nice it would be if you were to succeed, but force yourself to think about worst-case scenarios as well. Ask yourself "What if plan A fails? What if that one thing happens – that one thing that I find so scary I don't even want to think about it – but what if it happens? How will I solve it?" It is not nice to think about these questions, I know. But if you are able to answer them beforehand, it could save your life. You will have to imagine what you will do if everything around you fails, and rehearse your emergency plan so often that you are able to act it out in a split second if that is necessary.'

Negative thinking, however, is allowed only in the preparation phase of a project. 'During the performance itself,' Goodwin says, 'you have to let go of those thoughts. You won't need them any longer. In fact, if you held on to them for too long, they would make you afraid or stressed.' As soon as Goodwin starts climbing a building, he no longer allows negative thoughts to influence him. Or, at least he tries. 'Sometimes they travel along with me. If, during a climb, I see a crack in the glass of a window, and I can see that the glass has already rounded a little... that is typically a situation in which I go through that horror movie again. In my mind, I will see the glass splintering and myself falling backwards, my arms ploughing through the air... But if that happens during a climb I put a radical stop to it. The trick I do for that is to exchange the negative image, with a more positive one: mostly the one in which I can see myself on the top of a building. Tired, satisfied, proud. Goal reached.'

Not only does Goodwin exchange negative images for positive ones during his climbs, he combines them with positive affirmations. 'I repeat sentences in my head that make me feel sure of myself: "I can do this. I am strong. I am powerful." Usually I will turn around each negative thought that pops up in my head during an ascent, and replace it with its exact opposite. So, if I am thinking "I'm not going to make it", I replace that thought with "I will make it, I will succeed in this climb." If I'm thinking something like "my arms are getting pumped, I'm too weak to climb this building", I immediately replace that thought with another one: "I'm strong enough to reach the top. You know what? I might even go on and climb the antenna of this building, as well!".'

POSITIVE AFFIRMATIONS

Changing negative or fearful thoughts into positive affirmations is a skill that Goodwin has actively practiced over the past years. 'I've done it so often that it has now become second nature to me,' he tells me. 'I've trained myself to always be aware of any negative thoughts that I may have, even if I am not climbing. And it has become easy for me to replace them immediately with positive affirmations. The thing is: we're human beings, and all of us think negative thoughts every now and then. It's natural to us, you just can't avoid that. And like I said: I actually believe that negative thinking can be very useful, if it helps you to develop a Plan B, or an emergency plan. But most people don't use negative thoughts in that way. Instead, they start believing them and start acting them out. They think of a goal or wish, and think "Oh, that won't work out anyhow…" and then they give up before they have even tried making it work! See, that's the negative side of mental power. We can never completely control what we think, but we can train ourselves to deal with negative thoughts in a way that is constructive, rather than destructive.'

Goodwin knows many other extreme athletes who use similar methods. Stunt motor-cyclists who visualize in advance, BASE jumpers who think through what can go wrong. The reason why so many extreme athletes make use of these mental methods is that they have to act fast, Goodwin explains. After they have rehearsed their movements and decisions tens or hundreds of times in a visualization, they will be able to perform them in an almost mechanical way during their real-life race or flight. They will not doubt themselves under high stress: after all, they know that they will succeed – in their minds, they have already done so many, many times!

His method can also be useful in other situations. 'Say you have never been outside of the town where you were born and raised, and your dream is to make a trip to some exotic destination. There is a fair chance that this will excite you as much as it frightens you, as you don't know what to expect from your journey. Now, if you want to use the visualization method that I use, the trick is to think negatively, but not in a vague, concerned way, like "I hope everything goes well. Oh, what if things go wrong, what if I don't like it there, what if I become ill, what if the weather turns bad..." These are unhelpful thoughts. They are not concrete enough to help you develop a safety plan, and they are not positive enough to activate or empower you.'

He explains what a scared traveler should do: 'You start by thinking about your trip in the most realistic way. This means that you also visualize the things that could go wrong. You missing your flight, your luggage getting stolen. You getting ill from the exotic food. The next step is to think through the preparations you will need to make to solve those problems. One example might be making sure you have travel insurance. Or taking a copy of your passport with you, and a medicine kit. You think about the solutions until you know what you need to pack and do before you go; and then you rehearse how you will act once things go wrong.'

The difference between this positive and concrete approach to visualization and a more vague and negative one is that the former empowers you. Once you have been through this visualization process, nothing unexpected will happen during your journey. The worst that can happen is that something occurs that you have already been through and dealt with before – albeit in your mind.

'Step three of the method is to let go of the negative thinking. On your way to the airport you should only think positively, for example, "I am about to make a fantastic trip. I am going to enjoy myself." And you will not just think that, you will feel it, see it! You will envisage the success of your journey in detail: imagine yourself, with a big smile on your face and in a good mood, on that once-in-a-lifetime holiday.'

Or while climbing the highest building in the world.

CHAPTER 8

DON MCGRATH

'PERFORM AN ANALYSIS OF YOUR FEAR'

When I asked Don McGrath if he would be willing to be interviewed for a book on fear and higher performance, his reply was fast and encouraging, 'I'd love to! When do you have time to talk? Tomorrow?'

American climber and sports coach Don McGrath specializes in the mental aspects of climbing. He is also the author of several books and articles about top performance in the sport. His writings – and his willingness to contribute to this book – spring from a personal fascination with the feelings of fear and uncertainty that he experienced early in his climbing career.

MENTAL BLOCKS

McGrath started climbing when he was thirty years old. As the years passed, he climbed better and better, because he became physically stronger and perfected his technique. But, when he entered his forties, his progress seemed to stagnate. McGrath started to notice that he frequently under-performed. He had to give up at routes that, considering his physical fitness, should have been possible for him. He became convinced that his lack of success was not caused by physical weakness, but by some kind of mental weakness.

'It happened rather often that I gave up right before the top of a route', he recalls. 'At the very end, I would feel overwhelmed with tiredness or panic, and it would come into my head that I couldn't make it. While, at the same time, deep down inside, I knew I was good enough to succeed.'

McGrath sensed his lack of success had something to do with fear, with habits, with willpower... He was not yet clear about what it was that was bothering him, but he decided to find out.

He started his personal quest by collecting theories from psychological literature. He shared his findings on a blog, so that other climbers could read what he discovered.

'I started to experiment in practice with what I learned. Back then, my climbing buddy was Jeff Ellison, a professor in psychology. That proved to be very convenient for my research project! After I told Jeff what I was investigating, we decided to cooperate and eventually we wrote up our findings in a book, *Vertical Mind*.'

FEAR OF FALLING VS. FEAR OF FAILING

One of their main conclusions was that there are two types of fear that can hamper people's success: the fear of failing and the fear of falling. Someone who is afraid to fail does not to take on a challenge because he anticipates that he will not be able to succeed. A person who is afraid to fall, fears the consequences of a potential fall. Sometimes this fear is rational and sometimes it is not.

The two types of fear are most directly recognizable in the sport of climbing, McGrath argues. 'Climbers with a fear of failure won't even try a certain route, because they are convinced that they don't have a chance of reaching the top of the rock. They will stick to routes that are less challenging for them, in order to avoid failing. Climbers with a fear of falling will start hard routes, but they start panicking during the climb because they fear what might happen to them if they don't get the next move, and fall as a consequence.'

McGrath himself fell into the fear-of-failure category. While he mostly dared to start a challenging route, he would climb them half-heartedly. He did not manage to reach the top because he was convinced that he would not be able to. And so, again and again, he gave up.

The decision to give up was not the result of rational calculations, he emphasizes. 'A fear of failing is never rational. You are afraid that something might not work out well and therefore you give up before you've even tested that assumption. As such, you turn your fear into reality.'

Many other climbers struggle with a fear of falling. 'This fear can be irrational or rational. The rational aspect of a fear of falling in climbing is pretty obvious: if you fall during an ascent and you are not well protected, it is indeed possible to get hurt. You might even die. Yet most climbers are afraid in an irrational way: they are scared of falling even though they are well protected by a rope and other safety gear and can be sure that a fall would not cause them serious injuries. All that can happen is that they fly through the air for a couple of seconds, until the rope and the belayer catch them. That's a little alarming, but it's not dangerous. Nevertheless, climbers fear falling to such extent that they hyperventilate or lose focus due to their panic. They start moving more slowly, they get tired, pumped – and they give up. That is what we call the consequences of an irrational fear of falling.'

If a climber suspects that he is under-performing because of a mental obstacle, he first needs to investigate what type of fear is holding him back: of falling or failing. After that, he can start to overcome that fear. McGrath developed a fear-analysis method to help him do just that.

RISKS

Before introducing the analysis, let us briefly consider the difference between the fear of falling or failing in a non-climbing context. McGrath believes that non-climbers who under-perform are also usually bothered by one of these types of fears. 'I see this a lot with business leaders who doubt their decisions, and with people who dream about making a career switch, but do not dare to take the step.'

Asked for a concrete example of the way in which fear of falling can hamper success in a non-climbing context, McGrath asks me to imagine the following situation: 'For years, you have had a comfortable, well-paid job. But you have also developed an idea for a business of your own, that you would love to start up. This business is your passion. You would love to set it up, but you know that it would require you to quit your current job and lose your income. You have few savings, so your business will have to become successful soon or you will be in deep financial trouble. In this context, 'falling' would mean that you take the risk – you tell your boss you will no longer work for him and you start your own company. But, after some months of hard work with little success, you start to doubt that decision. Your financial concerns are distracting you to such an extent that you are unable to focus on the tasks ahead. You freeze, as it were, you find it hard to make new decisions, you don't know what to do and how to solve your problems, and eventually you give up.'

Compare that situation with the way in which fear of failing can stop a person from acting. 'In that case, you would be so afraid that your dream business will not thrive that you continue to work for your boss, even if you despise the job. The consequence is that you do not develop yourself, and that you feel bored and unhappy.'

McGrath's examples show that his advice to investigate what type of fear is holding you back, applies to climbers as well as to non-climbers. Are you afraid to switch careers because you doubt your own capacities, or because you fear that people in your social environment will criticize you if your business plan doesn't work out successfully? In both cases, it seems that the fear of failing is blocking your development, and it would be wise to work on strengthening your self-confidence. Or maybe you are convinced of your own capacities and are psyched to start up the business of your dreams, but you suspect that your product or service will not generate enough income. That is a fear of falling – and according to McGrath, that can be a very rational fear. 'Ending up broke and deep in financial problems could have serious consequences for a novice entrepreneur and his family. Just like a fall above a pointed piece of granite could seriously injure a climber. In both cases, people can get hurt, and the fear is rational.'

ANALYSIS

McGrath and his colleague Ellison developed a fear-analysis model that can help people understand the type of fear that is blocking their development. The model also provides an insight into the extent to which the fear is rational. 'Once you know that, it becomes much easier to take strategic decisions regarding your fear', McGrath promises.

In the analysis, the costs and benefits of a risky decision are evaluated on four different dimensions:

» the possibility of failing
» the consequences of failing
» the importance of reaching the goal
» the costs of giving up

For a climber, the fear analysis could look like this. Say a female climber is safely attached to a rope and finds herself halfway up a steep rock face. She is doing well and ascending steadily, but she is starting to get tired. She looks up, and discovers what she believes to be a difficult passage ahead. The fear of falling on that passage frightens her to such an extent that she starts hyperventilating. She is not certain whether she should proceed and risk falling, or give up now.

Enthusiastically, McGrath explains how his model could help the climber make a decision. 'First she considers the first factor, the possibility of failing. Is the passage really too complicated for her? Is she sure, because she has tried it before, or is she just thinking that this might be the case? And is she truly exhausted, or could she rest a little and gain strength?' If the climber decided that she has no reason to believe as yet that the passage will be too difficult for her, and if she could see an opportunity for her arms to get some rest, the conclusion of this first part of the analysis would be that the possibility of failing is not extremely high.

Factor two: the consequences of failing. The climber considers what might happen if she attempts to get through the passage and falls. In this case, the consequences of a fall would not be serious, argues McGrath. 'She is using safety gear and the face on which she is climbing is steep, meaning that, if she falls, she will not impact the rock and get injured, but will fall through the air.'

Factors three and four have to do with the urgency you feel to reach a certain goal. The climber asks herself how important it is for her to climb this route. Is this something for which she has trained for a long time, or would it be crucial for her self-confidence and development to make an attempt? Another way to ask this is to consider how she would feel afterwards, if she allowed herself to give up. Would she regret it deeply?

CONCLUSIONS

McGrath sounds confident when he shares his conclusion about his analysis with me: 'Based on the fear analysis, I would advise the climber to push through and risk the fall. That may be scary for her, but failing will not be unsafe physically. Plus, if she tries, she can be proud of herself for pushing her mental boundaries. While, if she backs out, she might end up with a feeling of disappointment.'

And what about the person doubting whether he should start his dream business? McGrath shows how he could apply the model. 'Factor one. This guy will have to estimate his risk of failing for his business. Say he performs a simple market analysis and finds there is little demand for the product or service he has to offer. Say, also, that he has been unable to find investors and no bank is willing to give him a loan. Then I would say that he runs a high risk of failing.'

Factor two: the possible consequences of failure. These will be less serious for a single person living in a cheap rental flat, than for the breadwinner of a family, with two children of school-going age and high monthly mortgage repayments.

'Say that the man from our case study is married and has children. In that case I would already advise him at this point of the analysis to stay put in his job. His chances of failing with the new business plan are obviously high, and the costs of failing are even higher. It would be much wiser for him to hold on to his current job until he has found a way to improve his business plan or save some more money.'

SCRIPTS

For those wondering what is wrong with making decisions on intuition, McGrath offers an interesting reply: the advantage of working with the fear-analysis method, rather than making risky decisions on the basis of gut feeling, is that it ensures that people do not make decisions out of habit. He explains that often, our fears do not reflect real dangers, but rather, our behavioral patterns and ideas.

The formal concept that psychologists use for this phenomenon is 'scripts': automatic, unconscious patterns of behavior and thought that we develop during our early life stages. Scripts are at work in the case of the adult who says 'no' to everything that is unknown to him, because as a child, he was never encouraged to try new things. They are also at work in the case of the woman who never dares to make a speech at work, simply because she never practiced speaking in front of an audience. And in the case of people who constantly make up new business plans but never execute them. Because they 'can't do that', or because they never did such a thing before, and now consider their plan insurmountable.

'A script can hamper someone's development without them being aware of it,' McGrath argues. 'We often see this with climbers: they believe that they are unable to climb certain routes because they consider them too steep or too technical – while they have never tried them before!'

That is a shame, he says, because by behaving according to a script, the climber does not allow herself to develop her skills – or surprise herself.

'A climber who feels afraid when considering trying a new route should try to gain an insight into her typical way of decision-making when she is confronted with unknown or intimidating routes. The same applies to people who are uncertain about some other frightening action. Are they uncertain out of habit or on the basis of a solid safety analysis? If the latter is true, if the action is truly risky, then it might be wise not to go ahead with it. But if the doubt springs from habit, then it would be worth exchanging the old script for a new one. The script of daring to fail safely, and fall safely!'

CHAPTER 9

EDURNE PASABAN

'LET YOURSELF BE GUIDED BY FEAR'

In 2010, Basque-Spanish mountaineer Edurne Pasaban Lizarribar (1973) became the first woman to climb the fourteen independent mountains on earth that are more than 26,247 feet above sea level. Only twenty males preceded her. Pasaban had climbed the first mountain in that list nine years earlier, and the expeditions that followed were not always easy. She has struggled with feelings of fear and doubt throughout her climbing career; more than once, she has felt forced to stop halfway through an expedition because she considered it too risky to continue. During her ascent of K2, the world's second highest mountain, Pasaban lost two toes and nearly froze to death after she had been outside in extreme cold weather conditions for over twenty-eight hours. She was saved by her expedition members.

A few years later, she would lose three close friends and fellow expedition members during an ascent, despite her efforts to save them. Theirs were not the last funerals of mountaineers she would attend in her life. 'At this moment, I have already lost fourteen close friends and colleagues,' she says. 'All of them died in the mountains. The reason I am still alive is not because I am a better climber. It is because I am a scared climber, and because I dare to act on the basis of my fear. Fear saved my life.'

INDUSTRIAL ENGINEER

Pasaban started mountaineering in her early teens, in the mountains and valleys of the Basque country, and felt that the sport came naturally to her. When she had turned fifteen, she took a course in rock climbing. A year later, she climbed Mont Blanc. A series of expeditions in the Andes and the Pyrenees followed, and hardly ten years later, in 1998, she had her first experience with mountaineering in the Himalayas. And it was a rather ambitious first experience, attempting to climb the seventh-highest peak of the world, in Nepal. The expedition had to be abandoned when weather conditions turned so bad that Pasaban and the other expedition members decided it would be too unsafe to continue to the top.

In that period of her life, although she devoted a lot of time and energy to mountaineering, she did not consider herself a professional climber. She was studying to become an industrial engineer, and was also doing a Master's course in Human Resource Management. Immediately after she had finished her studies, she took on a job as an engineer in her family's company, which manufactured paper cutters and winders. Later, while still working as an engineer, she started her own hotel and restaurant. The extra income helped her to pay for many expeditions into the mountains.

Things changed after she took part in a successful expedition to Mount Everest in 2001. Pasaban was 28 years old at the time, and hardly known in the climbing world. But when she returned from Everest, sponsors and other climbers suddenly knew her name. Personally, things had also changed. The Everest experience had made Pasaban, in her own words, 'addicted to the Himalaya'. Somehow, she knew she had to go back there. 'Climbing Mount Everest felt like a dream come true,' she says. 'Now I wanted more.' She started to think of herself as a professional climber, and with the help of sponsors, she was able to make yearly expeditions to high mountain peaks. Her climbs included Makalu, Cho Oyu and Lhotse in Nepal, and Gasherbrum I and 2 on the China-Pakistan border. Now in her thirties, Pasaban knew she had found her passion and lifestyle.

K2

And then, in the summer of 2004, her young climbing career – and her life – nearly came to an end. She had known beforehand that the ascent of K2 would be challenging. The mountain is known for its harshness and complexity and none of the six women who had tried to climb it before Pasaban had survived. The stories horrified her and made her nervous about her own attempt. Yet, at the same time, she felt determined to give it a try, and asked a team of experienced mountaineers to accompany her.

'I was a little afraid, but I also believed that my team had a fair chance of success,' she says. Pasaban and her team members talked extensively about the risks inherent to the expedition. And particularly about the difficult couloir – a narrow gully with a steep gradient – that they would have to cross, not too far from the top. They had calculated that, to reach the top before dark, they would have to arrive at the couloir around 1 pm. The group decided unanimously that, if they arrived at the couloir too late, they would not attempt to finish the climb. Moving in the dark would be way too dangerous; they would have to go back to base camp and accept their failure.

But during the climb, something else happened, a scenario that Pasaban and her colleagues had not foreseen. They arrived at the couloir on time, but the weather changed unexpectedly. A snowstorm made it impossible to see far ahead, and it took much longer than expected to cross the couloir. As a result, they arrived at the top of the mountain around 5 pm, many hours later than they had planned. According to their schedule, they should have started descending hours earlier. The team took no time to enjoy their success, and immediately hurried down. But Pasaban could not keep up. 'I was exhausted. I had spent way too much energy crossing the couloir. The others were moving faster than I was. At first, I could still see them walking in front of me, but before I knew it, I had lost sight of them.'

She trudged on for hours, a flashlight in her hand to help her find the way down. 'I remember one specific moment during my descent when I realized very clearly that I was in serious danger, that I might die. I don't remember what time it was exactly, but I think it was around 8 or 9 in the evening. I had lost the others hours before, and it was completely dark. The flashlight showed me where I to place my feet – until I dropped it. I still don't understand what made me drop it: maybe my fingers had become so cold that they could not hold on to it, or maybe I tripped, but in any case, the flashlight fell in a place where I could not reach it. So I had to continue walking without light. I can tell you that, on a high mountain like that, far away from cities and villages, it gets pretty dark.'

She shakes her head, as if she is still stunned by what happened to her, that night. 'The worst thing was that I knew I still had to pass a narrow part of the mountain. That was somewhere ahead of me, and I knew that it would be an extremely risky exercise without any light to help me. There was a serious risk that I would take a step too far, and fall over the edge.'

But she didn't panic. 'Instead, I stayed calm and started thinking very rationally. "I have to find the base camp", I thought, "and I will have to make my way down there very slowly, carefully".'

Pasaban descended by taking baby steps, but her body temperature became so low that her health deteriorated quickly. She was saved by her fellow expedition members just in time. When they finally found her after twenty-eigth hours and brought her to their base camp, Pasaban was already in a bad condition. In hospital, two toes had to be amputated and several other frozen body parts had to be treated medically.

'My mental state was even worse,' she tells me. 'I knew that I could be proud of myself that I had survived. Human beings apparently have a deep survival instinct that helps us remain calm in moments of crisis. I had always been afraid that something like this would happen to me in the mountains; that had given my nightmares! My experience on K2 showed me that I was able to stay calm and act rationally in such worst-case scenarios. I mean, if I had panicked, I would have died.'

DEPRESSION

But she was not proud of herself. Nor was she relieved that she had survived. She kept thinking back to that night on K2, and every time she did, she became sadder and more afraid. She realized that she would have died if other people had not saved her. And she blamed herself for what had happened. She dreamt about it, ruminated about it; eventually, the doctors declared that she was suffering from depression.

Pasaban was hospitalized for four months, struggling with fear and self-doubt. 'I was forced to think seriously about what climbing meant to me. I had become afraid, but I also longed for the mountains. Constantly, I asked myself questions. Would I dare to go back? Did I want to go back? Why, if I had experienced at first hand that the mountains could kill me? Perhaps the one question that kept coming back was this one: had I gone too far, was it my mistake that I nearly got killed on K2?'

Her answer to that last question was 'yes'. 'And it was very painful to come to that conclusion,' she says. 'See, this was the difference between my earlier experiences in the mountains and my ascent of K2: never before had I had to make a critical decision about whether or not to continue. It had always been obvious what to do: either the conditions were perfect, or they were so bad that there was no other option than to give up. I had told myself the story that I had been able to return safely from all of those climbs because I was a good decision-maker, someone who acted intelligently. But this time, it had been more complex. Things had felt vaguely wrong; it had not been obvious what to do. And, in hindsight, I had to admit that I had made the wrong decision when I told the team to continue to the top, after we had passed the couloir so slowly. In the hospital, I remembered that there had been a point when I had felt afraid, but I had ignored it, and pushed us through.'

She had ignored her gut feeling because she was ambitious, and wanted to reach the top. 'I wanted to succeed, no matter what. I should have given up: the weather conditions were bad, we were lagging behind schedule, there was a lot of snow. Yet I stubbornly continued. Now that I remembered that so clearly, I wasn't sure whether I could trust myself as a climber. Yes, I had remained calm at a critical moment and that may have saved my life, but it was my own behavior that had endangered my life in the first place.'

After the doctors declared her healthy and Pasaban left the hospital, she kept doubting whether or not to continue climbing. She was thirty-two years old, and she had come to realize that she had given up a lot of things in life to be in the mountains. 'I had spent all of my money and time on becoming a professional climber,' she tells me. 'I had no husband, no children, and nearly all my friends were climbers, too. And here I was, a woman with two amputated toes, who had nearly lost herself because she had come up against her boundaries – and crossed them. I recognized that choosing a climber's life, was choosing for a very lonely and risky life.'

The year after K2, she did not take part in any expeditions. 'Various climbing friends asked me to join their ascents in the Himalaya region, but I was too afraid.' But her friends eventually managed to persuade her to start climbing again. Pasaban smiles when she tells me about their passionate pleas: 'They told me: "Edurne, you love the mountains, the mountains are your life!" And I knew they were right. I had to go back to the mountains. But I still did not trust myself. So I decided that I would return with a new attitude. That would be the only way for me to overcome my fears.'

RESPECT YOUR FEAR

Pasaban promised herself that she would never, ever again ignore feelings of fear. Her experience on K2 had taught her a crucial lesson: to respect your fear. Now, the same shocking realization that she had nearly died due to her own bad decision-making became a relief to her. Pasaban understood that if she did not make the same mistake of ignoring her gut-feeling in future climbs, she could stay safe in the mountains. Her fear would protect her.

She believes that being afraid is a good thing. 'The adrenaline that comes with fear makes you attentive, sharp about what happens around you,' she says. 'That means you can act fast and rationally in moment of crisis, like I did when I was descending K2. And even more importantly: a deep-felt fear can provide you with immensely important advice. If something you plan to do truly frightens you, maybe that means you shouldn't go ahead with it. Listening to your intuition might save your life.'

Pasaban might have become convinced that listening to your fear is a good idea, but that opinion is not popular in the world of mountaineering. 'Most of my colleagues try their best to come across as if they are not afraid,' she says. 'Mountaineers generally like to show off about their bravery. We boast about the difficult and scary ascents that we have made. But the best mountaineers I know are the ones that allow themselves to be afraid every now and then, and then act accordingly. The climbers that suppress fear may be successful up to a certain point, but there will be a time that they don't return safely to their base camp. They make bad decisions, they overestimate themselves, like I did on K2.'

But, I suggest, even listening to your intuition doesn't take away all the risks inherent to climbing mountains of over 26,000 feet high. What if a storm comes up so suddenly that there is no time to be afraid? And what if a piece of rock breaks and lands on your head? Pasaban admits that mountaineering involves risks that can't be taken away by any mental attitude. 'But we all face challenges in our lives. Mountaineers face them up high; people who do not climb may face them in different situations. But they will face risks and difficult situations, probably types of risk that I will not face, because I am away in the mountains. Maybe they drive in cars more often than I do. So we all have personal risks in our lives, and other people will never be able to decide for you what is the best way to go about them. It is up to you to get to know your own gut feeling, and to decide what risks you find worth taking, and what not. That philosophy brought me back into the mountains.'

FOURTEEN PEAKS

Her return to the mountains did not evolve gradually. Pasaban got back on track with a new plan: to climb all of the world's mountains that are higher than 26,000 feet, fourteen in total. She starts laughing when she sees my surprised face, and says 'I had never considered such an idea before in my climbing career. I just picked mountains that attracted me, without any strategic plan. But now this idea appealed to me. It is as if my accident stimulated me to take myself more seriously as a professional climber. I knew now where my personal boundaries were – the moment I would get very afraid, I knew I had to stop. And so I knew that by following that rule, I would be able to climb the world's highest mountains in a relatively safe manner. I would return safely because I would no longer be guided by blind ambition or the wish to be brave and successful, but by my fear.'

So, I ask, did having this new attitude mean that she no longer doubts herself in the mountains? Pasaban shakes her head and gestures how wrong I am for thinking that. 'The rest of my climbing career I have had many fearful moments. I doubt myself, things frighten me – and I cherish that. Precisely all those feelings have been keeping me safe! I went back to K2, several years after my accident, and I was much more scared than during my first attempt. But now, I took that feeling seriously. I looked at it, tried to understand what it was telling me. It told me to stay alert, but to move on. And this time I got to the top, and descended safely.'

And so it went with the other mountains on her list. 'My intuition guides me and keeps me safe, each and every time. Take the expedition that I undertook with a team of Italian climbers. We got to a traverse, a crossing, that looked dangerous. It was late, I was tired. And we didn't have a rope with us, because we had anticipated beforehand that the traverse would not be too complicated for us. Now, looking at it from close-up, I felt we couldn't take the risk. I figured we would probably be able to cross the traverse safely, but it would cost us a lot of energy. So much that we might not make it back. Oh, I didn't like the feeling that told me not to keep going! After the traverse, it would only be 656 feet to the top! But my fear told me "no". My expedition members tried to convince me. "Edurne, let's just do it", they argued. "This will be easy for us!" But I stuck to my decision.' That was not hard for her, she now recalls, as her gut feeling was clear to her. The others went anyhow, without her. 'I told them I would wait for them. And one of them never returned. What happened to him was exactly what I had feared: he crossed the traverse, reached the top, but got so tired and cold during the descent that he died.'

To Pasaban, the only reason she is still alive and so many climbers are not, is that she lets her fear guide her. And that is the advice that she wants to give to anyone who is faced with a serious challenge in life: listen to your intuition. 'Take your fears seriously. They protect you.' That doesn't mean that you have to give up on dreams that scare you, Pasaban emphasizes. But it might mean that you have to postpone your goal for a while. 'I hardly ever give up on a set goal, not even if it frightens me. Sometimes, if I am climbing, I am unable to reach the top in one attempt, for example when the weather turns bad. I see dark clouds, I get afraid, and so I turn around and find safety in the base camp. But I always promise myself at those moments that one day, I will return and try again. That may be a day later, when the wind has dropped, or it may be a year or two later. But I will go back. And again. And again. As often as is necessary to reach my goal, without disrespecting my fear. I have become the first women to climb all eight-thousanders in the world by using this strategy, so the fact that I allow my fear to guide me, has not made me at all unsuccessful.'

CHAPTER 10

JORG VERHOEVEN

'APPROACH YOUR GOAL SYSTEMATICALLY'

A COUPLE OF WEEKS AFTER I have sent Dutch sport climber Jorg Verhoeven (32) a request for an interview, I still haven't heard from him. I give it a second try – nothing. And then suddenly, another week or so later, a Facebook message pops up on my screen; Jorg is climbing in an area where he rarely has an internet connection, but he'll get back to me! And off he goes again. But he sticks to his promise and does get back to me a month or so later. We talk over Skype, because he has settled down in Austria for the time being and does not expect to return to the Netherlands any time soon. 'There's too much to climb here', he tells me.

Jorg Verhoeven (1985) is probably the most well-known sport climber in the Netherlands but, while he excelled at competition climbing, bouldering and sport climbing, he has now also become one of the climbing elite, topping out some of the world's hardest big-wall free routes.

He has been participating in indoor climbing competitions since his early teens, and won many of them. In 2001, when he had just turned sixteen years old, he became world champion in his age category. Since then, he has steadily improved his climbing skills and has now climbed routes in the upper 5.14 difficulty grade range (9a, in the French grading system); and he even succeeded in climbing a bigwall route graded at

Chapter 10 - Jorg Verhoeven

5.14, the *Dihedral Wall* in Yosemite, USA (for non-climbers: that grade is unimaginably hard, and only climbers with an extremely good technique, balance and power are able to attain it!)

THE NOSE

In 2014, Verhoeven was the first European to free climb the iconic route 'The Nose' – on the massive granite wall El Capitan, in Yosemite. 'Free climbing' means that a climber is allowed to use rope and other safety gear to protect himself from falling, but not to make the ascent easier or faster. Free climbing The Nose is an enormous achievement. Each year, on average, 400 to 600 climbers try to climb The Nose; very few of them try to do so 'free'. For years, almost none of those aspiring free climbers succeeded – and then Verhoeven drove up to Yosemite in his van. The van was filled with ropes, carabiners, harnesses and climbing shoes; his head with ambitious dreams.

For a long time, The Nose was regarded as unsurmountable. That perception changed in 1967, when Warren Harding and a team of fellow climbers tried to ascend with a new climbing technique. They used hammers, nails and other materials to haul themselves up. In between the climbing, they rested in a sort of tent, which they attached to the wall. They got to the top in forty-five (!) days.

In the years that followed, many different climbers tried to get to the top of The Nose – preferably faster than Harding and without using so many materials. In 1993, American climber Lynn Hill (see chapter 12 of this book) was the first to free climb The Nose. It took her three days. One year later, she repeated the climb, this time within twenty-four hours. That achievement was hard to beat – between 1994 and 2014 only two more climbers managed to free climb the nose. Hundreds of others had to give up halfway. And then it was Verhoeven's turn.

'Ever since I was a kid it has been a dream for me to climb The Nose', he tells me. He speaks calmly and thoughtfully. After every question, he takes the time to think through his answer, which he then formulates precisely. 'But I also knew how difficult it would be to free climb this wall. I had heard so many stories about the failed attempts of other strong climbers, and was aware that there are a variety of challenges in climbing The Nose.'

The main challenge is not so much the complexity or difficulty grade of the wall, but its length. Although The Nose is not exactly an easy wall to climb, for good and experienced climbers it should be technically possible. The problem is that they will have to maintain their good level of climbing for 2,900 feet in a row. And *that* is challenging, explains Verhoeven: 'A lot of the climbers who made an attempt before me were very good climbers and they had succeeded at many other projects. But with this one, they gave up. Sometimes because they became physically tired after a few days of climbing, but even more often, they lose their motivation along the way, or their focus.'

If a climber loses focus, he risks slipping. 'A couple of sections on the wall are famous for their slickness. The rock feels slick and slippery, there is hardly any structure to hold on to. It's easy to lose your balance if you are not completely concentrated, and then your feet slip off. That is what makes The Nose so hard and interesting at the same time: you don't have to be particularly strong to get to such sections, but you have to be able to move precisely, to not make mistakes. For that you need to be completely concentrated – all the many hours you are climbing the wall.'

Once a climber has managed to do that for nearly 2,900 feet and he is reaching the top, he will meet another challenge. This is the crux, the most difficult part of the route. 'When you get there you are exhausted, physically and mentally,' Verhoeven recalls, 'and then you have to be able to give it all.' He was able to do just that – most other climbers are not.

BIG WALL

Besides the length and the crux move near the top, The Nose has one other main challenge for its wannabe-climbers: it requires complex organization. For a 'big wall' climb such as The Nose, climbers usually spend several days on the wall. This means they sleep and rest in a portaledge, a sort of tent that you can attach to the wall. From the portaledge, they haul up rope and other gear, as well as kilos of food and water. That way, they don't have to carry it with them while they are climbing. But the hauling itself demands physical strength and a certain skilfulness that not all climbers have.

While aware of the fact that so many climbers before him failed in their attempt, Verhoeven dared to dream big and felt confident that he had a good chance of free climbing The Nose. His secret weapon was his ability to approach goals systematically and rationally. That strategy has helped him to succeed in all of his projects, no matter how insurmountable they may seem.

His approach starts by testing assumptions. The idea that, if others were not able to climb The Nose, then he would not be able to do it either, is a perfect example of such an assumption. 'Of course, at some point, it crossed my mind. But there is no evidence for that belief, and it is based only on things that I have heard about other climbers' attempts, not on concrete information.' As soon as it crossed his mind, Verhoeven decided he would refuse to give up his dream of climbing The Nose for a hardly-convincing assumption. Instead, he would research the facts and then make a rational estimation of his realistic chances.

RESEARCH

Verhoeven started to talk to climbers who had attempted to climb The Nose, and started reading online articles about their attempts. It was through this research that he discovered that each of them had to give up not because they weren't fit or strong enough, but because they lacked the willpower or motivation to push through. In a way, that was comforting for Verhoeven. 'Knowing myself, I know I have strong willpower,' he says. 'And I was able to use a lot of that for this project. I also felt I was willing to spend much time and energy on it. So, if for others mental power had been the main problem that prevented them in reaching their goals, I knew I naturally had in me what it takes to climb this wall.' That rational analysis did not guarantee his success, but it was convincing enough for him to turn his dream into a serious goal.

The second step of his approach was to make a detailed plan and time schedule for how to go about it. In this planning, he worked from a specific mindset: one in which he anticipated that this would become a long-term, complex, energy-sapping project. One in which he would have to take lots of time to sort out the organization and practice, and in which he needed to remain utterly aware of his motivation. So the schedule that he eventually made for himself did not just set out the time frame (when he would travel to Yosemite, what would be the best season to climb there) and the practical preparations (which gear to take, which physical training he would do to prepare his body for this particular route), but even more so the mental aspects of this goal. He noted that this adventure would cost him more time, power and energy then he had ever had to use for his climbing. And he was ready to spend it.

After gathering all the information that he needed in his research phase, and reflecting on what he thought he would need for a successful attempt, Verhoeven decided that he would need a month in Yosemite to have a fair chance of success. That would give him time to practice the most difficult sections of the route in isolation from the other parts of the wall – which, he hoped, would help him to keep his motivation higher when he tried to climb the whole thing at once – and it would allow some time for failure. If things did not go as fast as he now hoped, he would still have some time left to accomplish his goal. And that would save him time-stress.

It might be an open door, says Verhoeven, but making a good plan is crucial for reaching goals. And many people under estimate what is needed to make their dream come true, either in time, in gear, or in the training they need to do in preparation.

SYSTEMATIC

He sounds almost apologetic when he speaks about the ways in which he plans to achieve his goals: 'I typically work towards them in a very systematic way, because I am convinced that realistic planning increases your chances for success. Really thinking through your plan may take you a little more time than you may be used to at the beginning of a project, but it will save you time later. It helps you to avoid miscalculations. See, there are many factors that can hamper your plans. Take the weather. If it rains, the rock gets wet and slippery. If the sun has been shining for weeks, the rock becomes too hot to climb. Clearly, any climber has to think about the weather when making a plan for a project. It might mean that you travel to the mountain you want to climb in a dry and not-too hot season. Or, if a full agenda makes that impossible, it might mean that you add some extra days to the time you think you would need to climb it, so that even if it rains, and you cannot climb for a day or two, you have sufficient time left to reach the top.

A similar systematic approach works well in a non-climbing context. 'Thinking through what you want to do, and what you realistically need for that, measured in time, money, practice or other relevant things: in my opinion that is the best way to go for pretty much every big project. For a holiday, for example, or a big work deadline you have to catch. The way in which I plan for climbing is not so different from preparing yourself for another challenge in life.'

In 2014, Verhoeven was ready to execute his plan. He travelled to Yosemite, where he found dry and shaded rocks – according to plan. He also found a rock face that was even steeper and more intimidating than he had imagined beforehand, but that was no reason for panic or self-doubt. He had a full month to get to know The Nose, practice on it and – eventually – conquer it.

Verhoeven started practicing the crux passage, near the top. He would hike to the top of the wall via the not-so-steep side of the mountain, pitch a tent, set up a self-belay in the rock, and lower himself on a rope to the sections in the route that he expected to be most difficult. He practiced all day until he was too tired to do any more, then fell asleep in his tent on the top.

After days of practicing, he felt he could get through the crux passage quite easily, and he moved down to other difficult segments lower down. Starting from the base of the mountain this time, he experienced how difficult it is to keep your motivation up. 'Some of the lower parts were much harder than I had expected. Some days I was hardly making any progress at all. I would try and try and fail every time. I just couldn't understand how anyone was ever able to ascend here. I stared for hours at the wall in the evenings, and fell asleep exhausted and full of self-doubt. But the next morning I would start practicing again. Once in a while, I suddenly succeeded in a certain move, or finally got through a difficult section. That kept my hopes up.'

FIRST ATTEMPT

After three weeks in Yosemite, Verhoeven had managed to free climb all the difficult sections in the wall. Now he was ready to climb the whole thing at once. After he had found a belayer, they waited for perfect weather, and the two of them began their journey upwards.

Verhoeven and his belayer stayed on the wall for three days. They climbed, ate and slept. Verhoeven was climbing well. He got through the difficult sections without too many problems, and neared the top – and the crux – quite quickly. He felt confident, felt he would succeed. And then things became gloomier. Even though he had practiced the crux passage many times, this time he couldn't get through. He reached for a piece of rock, but couldn't get a good hold of it. He fell in the rope.

He recalls how, at that moment, he was overwhelmed with self-doubt. 'Thoughts tumbled through my mind. I had performance anxiety, feared that maybe I had been wrong, maybe I would not succeed after all.' What saved him from giving up or panicking was, once more, his systematic approach. 'I stopped climbing for a bit, took a break. Hanging in the rope, I made a new rational analysis of my chances. I thought back to the weeks before, when I had been practicing this move. The fact that I had been able to do it then proved that my technique was good enough. The idea that I had suddenly lost my technical skills seemed absurd. It was much more likely that I was tired, and maybe my performance was suffering from the pressure that I felt to succeed.' Realizing what was hampering him from success helped Verhoeven to regain confidence. 'I told myself that the insecurity that I was feeling, was unnecessary and illogical,' he says. 'There were many more reasons to believe that I could do it than to believe I couldn't.'

He looked at the rock above him, repeated in his mind the moves that he would have to make to get through the crux section, and did it. 'For me as a climber, it is extremely important to stay positive. That also applies to non-climbers; to everyone who is working to reach a goal and meeting challenges. You cannot let yourself be overtaken by self-doubt and negative thoughts that are based on assumptions, not facts. If you allow that to happen, you will lose motivation, and you will give up. But if you stick to the conclusion that you draw on the basis of your rational calculations and your solid planning, you will reach your goal. For me, I got through that crux that second time because rational thinking helped me to get my self-trust back. I knew I could do it, and so I could.'

A few minutes later, he stood on the top of El Capitan. Mission accomplished. Exactly within the thirty days he had reserved for the project. 'I felt proud and happy. Or, actually...those emotions came only later. At that moment, I was mainly exhausted.'

CHAPTER 11

HAZEL FINDLAY

'STRENGTHEN YOUR FEAR-MUSCLE'

At the moment the interview for this book takes place, British climber Hazel Findlay (28) is unable to do what she likes best, since she has recently undergone an operation on an old climbing injury in her shoulder. According to her doctors, the recovery could take up to a year. That is not good news for someone who has been climbing since she was seven years old and who wrote in her blog that climbing is one of the only things in life that makes her truly happy.

'Oh well,' Findlay says, matter-of-factly. 'The advantage is that I have all the time in the world now to reflect on the themes of fear and climbing. You've picked a perfect period to talk to me. Normally I travel and train a lot and I don't have time to study on such themes, while at the same time they do fascinate me. People who see me climbing often think I'm extremely brave, or that I was born without any fear of heights. But I've very often been afraid when I was climbing. And sometimes I go through phases of not being confident in my own ability. I'm in one of those phases at the moment because I'm just coming out of this injury and I'm a bit unsure about how well I can climb.'

TRADITIONAL CLIMBING

That doesn't mean that she is not determined to get back on the rocks as soon as she can. Findlay never takes the easy way out. She is known to prefer climbing routes that are technically complex, and climbs them with a style known as 'trad climbing', which is regarded as riskier than the more popular sport climbing.

In trad climbing, climbers themselves place all the gear required to protect them against falling (known as 'protection'), and remove it again when a pitch is complete. That means searching for cracks or holes in the rock, and running the risk of falling a long way if you don't find them in time or if the protective gear doesn't stay in place in the rock. That is very different from sport climbing, where climbers can use bolts and permanent anchors fixed in the rock.

Findlay's climbing career reflects a fascinating duality. She has often been afraid of falling during climbs, yet she also takes on challenges that other climbers stay away from because they think they are too scary, too hard, or too long - like her technically complicated ascent in Morocco, which entailed climbing for sixteen hours non-stop. But Findlay 'just likes that kind of stuff', even though she admits that what she does can be pretty scary.

'Sometimes the rock is so compact that you can't find a place to fix your protection. I actually run into that problem a lot, because of my length.' Findlay is only five feet two. 'That means I often can't reach a crack or a hole in the wall that a taller climber could reach. Then all I can do is to keep climbing up, until I see somewhere that I can place my protection, and stand comfortably and safely while I do it.'

It can take a long time for Findlay to find a good spot. 'If you're already ten feet or more above your last protection point, and you realize that if you will fall, you will fly tens of feet through the air before the rope catches you... then you get scared. And you start thinking: what will be the physical consequences if you fall? Will you smack into the rock, will you fall painfully hard in your harness? Once that mental process starts, you can become so afraid that you lose all control over your body and mind,' says Findlay.

It has happened to her a few times. And, she predicts, 'it will happen to me many more times in the future. In a few months, when my shoulder injury has healed enough for me to start training again, there's no doubt I'll be scared! The first few times I'm back on the rock, I won't only be out of shape physically, but mentally, too. So I need to train both my body and my mind.'

FEAR-MUSCLE

Findlay's training routine is different than what you might expect from an athlete. For one, she does not visit the gym very often. She is also not into strict dieting, and has only followed a structured physical training scheme once. 'Let's just say that committing to physical training is not one of my strongest points,' she says, grinning. 'Most climbing coaches would probably say I should do some weight-lifting to make my arms stronger. But I don't feel like doing that.'

Is her mental power then maybe her greatest strength? 'Not at all!' Now she laughs out loud. She may often be portrayed as a daredevil in the media, but Findlay doesn't recognize herself in that description at all. 'I'm not an extraordinarily brave or fearless climber. Maybe the better the climber you are, the more you have had conversations about fear with yourself. Therefore, the better you become with dealing with stress. I'm not sure how much that equates to my natural ability to deal with fear, or to another persons' ability to deal with fear. It's just that my idea of what is risky, and what is fearful, is different. And that comes through experience. The reason I'm a successful climber is that I have trained myself to deal with being afraid. I actually practice that a lot.'

Findlay describes the capacity to cope or overcome fear almost as though it were a muscle: a part of the human body, like your biceps, that can be strengthened if used regularly. 'Yes, you could say that I train my fear-muscle a lot. That definitely helps me to climb sketchy routes or to do other exciting things in my life. And it's an easy enough method – everybody can use it to learn and dare to do more.'

Findlay argues that in climbing, there is much more attention to physical training than to mental tools. And that is strange, she says, because 'for most people, climbing *is* scary. Even professional climbers often get scared! Believe me, there are only very few people in the world who never experience fear of falling or heights. It's logical to feel scared if you are high up somewhere and know you can fall and fly through the air any moment. We humans weren't made to climb up high or to fly through air. We didn't develop wings, we have legs to walk with instead. From an evolutionary perspective, when we were still hunters, we probably learned to be afraid of high areas because we risked hurting ourselves if we fell. So, we preferred to stay low down, at ground level. That makes complete sense. And now, in our current lives, we still experience that fear of heights if we want to go to high places, for example, to go rock climbing. Biology tells us 'this is not normal!' And that's where the problems start: as soon as we move too high up, our bodies start giving us warning signals. Your knees start trembling, you start breathing more quickly and you want only one thing: to get down as soon as possible.'

ACCEPTING FEAR

Most of us, anyway. Findlay has always felt drawn to heights, as much as she is aware of their risk. She loves climbing, and is convinced that it is the greatest sport there is. But her biggest fear is falling and injuring herself during an ascent. It is an ambiguity that she has experienced since she first went climbing. 'If you want to push yourself in climbing, especially trad climbing, you have to accept fear as part of that'.

The fear to get injured after a bad fall is particularly strong when she has not spent much time climbing, for example after another cold, British winter, when she usually trains in low, indoor gyms. After weeks of indoor practice, her first climbs outdoors feel very uncomfortable. She gets ten feet up and starts to doubt whether her belayer is paying attention, twenty feet up and she is afraid that she will hurt herself crashing against the rock if she falls...

For Findlay, after a cold season or an injury, there is only one thing that she can do to overcome this fear and reach the top: she has to strengthen her fear-muscle all over again. 'I will have to get my body and mind used to the experience of being high above my bolt and being afraid of a fall that might hurt me. That is what I mean by training your fear-muscle. Just like we train our physical muscles, first we essentially break them down a bit first, we stress them, and then afterwards, they grow and we build them. It's the same with our mental training, in learning how to deal with stress. You have to put yourself in a stressful position, not so stressful that it injures your mind, just like you wouldn't hurt your body. And then that bubble of what you deem to be a comfortable situation, grows.'

In psychological terms, the technique that Findlay recommends to manage fears is rehearsal of performance under mild stress – a method also used by Alex Honnold (chapter 2 of this book). It consists of regularly putting yourself into scary situations, situations that make you feel anxious, nervous or stressed, explains Findlay. 'You can consciously look for such situations in life, and you should, if you want to learn how to overcome fear.'

MAINTENANCE

Findlay considers strengthening the fear-muscle a crucial and constant aspect of her training. 'Your ability to manage fears needs maintenance. Otherwise it will weaken again.' To ensure her fear-muscle does not weaken, Findlay trains it as often as she can, for example as part of her warm-up routine at the beginning of the outdoor climbing season, before starting a climb.

Her training method consists of two steps. Firstly, she will select a rock face that is not too high and not too scary. She agrees with her belayer that she will practice falling into the rope. She starts climbing, and after ten feet or so, she will let go of the rock just above a protection point. She will make a short fall and feel that her belayer and the rope catch her safely. She will repeat that exercise a couple of times, long enough for her to notice that she no longer feels scared when she falls. By repeating this simple exercise, her body learns that falling will not hurt her in any way. Another advantage of this exercise has to do with her state of mind: by falling and being caught safely again and again, Findlay becomes convinced that her belayer is paying attention and is capable of catching her. That increases her confidence that, later, in a more difficult route, the belayer will catch her safely too if she makes an unexpected fall.

In step two of her fear-muscle training, Findlay increases the length of the fall. This time, she climbs all the way to the top of the rock, placing protection as she goes up. But she purposely skips the protection point at the top. As soon as she gets there, she lets go of the rock, falling backwards for several feet until her fall is blocked by the first protection point below her. 'Again, the first time I do this, it feels scary. But the more often I practice it, the less scary it feels. It will get to a point where

I feel calm and in control while climbing and falling.' And that means she is ready to climb – for real.

DRIVING A CAR

Findlay believes that her training method is not just useful in climbing, but that it can also help people to cope with other situations where they are afraid. 'I'm convinced that training your fear-muscle can help you do things that scare you in many other moments in life. Just think of the first time you ever drove a car. Do you remember how scary that was? I know I was terrified! Everything is so new, it goes so fast, and you have to think about doing everything the instructor tells you to do. You doubt your own capabilities – will you ever be able to learn how to drive this thing? But then, after an hour or so of practicing, you've got a bit used to the speed and you're starting to understand how the clutch works. The next lesson, you will still feel nervous, but you already believe that you will be able to learn without causing a major accident. And years later, after many hours of practice, you will step into the car every morning without even thinking of the risk. You have got used to the speed and the action of driving to such an extent that it feels natural to you, and you no longer feel any fear at all!' In other words, drivers strengthen and maintain their fear-muscle by driving regularly.

Findlay stresses the importance of keeping it up, 'What if you suddenly stop driving, for whatever reason? For twenty years, you don't go near a car. Then there's a good chance that you will feel anxious all over again when you do sit behind the wheel again. That's because your fear-muscle has weakened. You will have to train it regularly again, so that it becomes strong enough to control your fear.'

Findlay gives another example from everyday life in which the fear-muscle approach can be useful. 'Imagine a person who is super shy, and who feels uncomfortable whenever she finds herself in a big social group. She could train her fear-muscle by first inviting a few good friends to her home for some drinks or dinner. Maybe two, maybe three or four people – just enough for her to feel slightly nervous about it in anticipation of their arrival. But hopefully, and most likely, she will feel that the evening turns out okay, and maybe she can even enjoy the presence of her friends a little. The next step would be to meet this same group of friends in a low-key bar. She repeats until that feels comfortable. And the final step would be to meet her friends in a busy spot, where there are a lot of other people around.'

DON'T OVERSTRETCH

But there is one great risk with Findlay's training method: like a physical muscle, the fear-muscle can become overstretched if you push it too hard. 'You can challenge yourself by putting yourself into a position where you feel slightly uncomfortable. But never force yourself to be in a situation where you feel complete panic. If you push your boundaries too fast, your body will learn to associate that particular situation with outright fear. The next time you try it, your body's stress signals will only have worsened and it will be impossible to concentrate and perform well, let alone experience any kind of fun. And why would you keep doing something that brings you nothing but a negative experience?'

In such situations, you have injured your fear-muscle, and you are worse off than when you started your training. To keep you fear-muscle strong and healthy, don't force yourself to drive across a busy intersection if you haven't driven a car for years, and don't visit a club with loud house-music and sweaty, dancing people if the idea of your grandmother's birthday party already makes you nervous. Instead, find that sweet spot in the middle where what you are going to do is a little bit scary, but is still fun.

While overstretching your fear-muscle is not advisable, not training it at all may be even worse, says Findlay. According to her, if you live without experiencing fear at all, you miss out on the best moments in life. 'Of course, there are people who avoid doing anything that frightens them. They live a life that is determined by their fears, not by their deepest wishes and longings. But I don't believe most people would like to live that type of life. There is a reason why so many of us enjoy visiting theme parks in our holidays – because we get that adrenaline kick, after we have overcome our own fears and stepped into that rollercoaster that looked so scary. And people like that feeling. If there was no adrenaline kick, if biology wasn't saying 'this is not normal', then people would just get bored. So even though we find many things in life scary, at the same time we are attracted by exactly those things. That is why, after my shoulder has recovered, I will start climbing again – even if that means that I will have to cope with my fears. I am prepared to train and work hard for that goal, because I know that once I've gained control over my fears and I am again able to climb without too much anxiety, then I will feel at my best.'

CHAPTER 12

LYNN HILL

'STOP. ACCEPT. REFRESH YOUR MIND. CONTINUE'

The American climber Lynn Hill is a living legend in the climbing world. She is small (just under five feet two), does not appear particularly muscular, but has climbed rocks that huge muscular men could not imagine possible. John Long, an ex-boyfriend and fellow climber, describes her as: 'The biggest little hero I've ever known.' Hill has changed climbing: she has done things that others believed were impossible, such as her free climb of the most famous big wall in the world, 'The Nose' in El Capitan in Yosemite Valley, California.

Hill was born in Detroit in 1961 and grew up in California. It was there where she climbed for the first time. Her older brother and sister took her climbing for the first time at the age of fourteen. Quickly it became apparent that Lynn had a lot more talent than her siblings, and at the age of sixteen she set out with her first boyfriend who she met in Yosemite Valley, to climb higher, steeper and more complicated rocks. Holidays, weekends and evenings: Hill spent all her free time climbing. For weeks on end, she and a group of climbing fanatics slept in cars, vans and tents near the rocks. They lived off little, mainly ate food out of tins and warmed themselves for hours in nearby cafes with mugs of coffee.

STUNTWOMAN

For the first part of her stay in Yosemite, Hill was known as the

Chapter 12 - Lynn Hill

'girlfriend of' the much more experienced climber John Long, the man mentioned above, but that was soon to change. In 1979, at the age of nineteen she became the first woman and possibly the first American to climb a route with a difficulty level of 5.13a (7C+, in French climbing grades). She crashed onto the international sport climbing scene, which was at that time becoming increasingly organized, and won more than thirty competitions.

Lynn's talent and daring were noticed in the climbing world and beyond. She was asked to take part in television productions like 'Survival of the Fittest', where various athletes competed against each other in sports such as climbing and cross-country running. Hill won four seasons in a row, beating several Olympic athletes on the way. She got paid work doing dangerous stunts on television (for example, viewers could see Hill climb over a hot air balloon while it hovered 6000 feet above the ground) and appeared in many TV shows.

Often Hill complained vehemently about the discrimination inside the climbing world that she experienced as a woman. Hill talked about the derogatory remarks that she sometimes heard from men, saying that they did not believe she could climb as well as they could, and about the difference in how male and female performance in competitions was valued. She consistently called for more women to start climbing. If Hill had succeeded in this, should there not have been more women able to climb at a high level? But that was easier said than done: Hill was extremely good, and there were only a few women who could equal her. Nevertheless, Hill – and the fact that she as a female climber was so much in the picture – was seen as one of the instigators of rock climbing's growing popularity among women in the 1980s.

Sponsors saw her media appearances too, and from the end of 1980s, Hill was formally paid to climb. But only on rocks: Hill swore she would never climb hot air balloons again, because looking back she named it 'possibly the most ridiculous stunt that I have ever done'.

Hill travelled all over the world, and lived for several years in France and Italy to climb famous cliffs there. Mostly she did this successfully: she became the first women in the world to climb a route with a difficulty grade of 5.14b (8b+, in the French climbing grades) and that is no easy feat.

PAUSE

But even in successful careers such as that of Hill there are moments of stagnation or setbacks. When she was twenty-eight years old she survived a fall of over seventy-two feet in Buoux, France, because she had not finished tying into the rope in order to walk over to where her shoes were sitting. During her preparation at the foot of the cliff before setting off on what appeared to be an easy climb, she was distracted by a conversation with another climber who was passing by. Once Hill got to her anchor, she leaned back to allow herself to be lowered down by her belayer (and her husband at the time), but instead of feeling tension of the rope on her body, she just felt air.

Hill hit a tree, and fell through it to the ground, where she landed between two rocks. She came out of it relatively well, with 'only' a broken ankle, a seriously dislocated arm, and dozens of bruises, cuts and scratches. That was possibly her most important climbing and life experience ever – and she learned a lifelong lesson: 'If you are at a difficult point on the way toward your goal, and if you face an enormous challenge and you're not sure you can do it, it's crucial that you make sure to pause for a moment before becoming overcome by doubts and fear. Stop resisting and accept how you feel, pause long enough to get your head together, and then continue climbing when it feels right.'

It took Hill some months to physically recover. In the recovery period she thought a lot about her mistake, about climbing and how important it was for her. She started to train again and travelled back to Europe to compete on the World Cup Circuit. After several years of climbing and training for competitions, Hill decided to retire from the realm of competition climbing and return to the US, ready for new adventures.

In 1993 she became the first person to free-climb The Nose; then she did it in three days, but a year later she repeated the feat in just twenty-four hours. She is now fifty-six years old, still climbs, and is seen as one of the best climbers – female or male – ever.

'Climbing has taught me to how to deal with challenges. It has allowed me to understand that, *en route* to our end goal, we often start panicking because we get signals from our body that it is not going to be successful. And from these signals we deduce that the end goal is indeed unreachable; through that we become scared or start to doubt ourselves, and finally we give up. But that is completely unnecessary'. At least, not if you employ Hill's success strategy, which she sums up as 'stop, accept and regroup'.

Hill gives an example of the manner in which physical stress signals can stop you achieving an objective during a climb: 'First you notice that your arms begin to feel a little tied or "pumped" in the jargon of climbers. Then you get afraid from that physical stress signal, and you start to think you are not able to reach the top without falling. Your arms feel so heavy, and your muscles start to cramp up more, and you still have a long way to go ...' In fact the climber still has all chance of success in this situation: cramping arm muscles only need a short time to recover. Yet the doubt that attacks the climber means that the chance of success diminishes. The belief that the battle is already lost makes it difficult to keep performing well.

SELF-FULFILLING PROPHECY

This is, according to Hill, an example where the interpretation of a physical experience can influence our performance in a positive or negative way. 'I have been thinking a lot about this in recent years. People believe that certain conditions are necessary to achieve their goals. If my foot slips on the crux of my red point ascent, I may or may not fall. If that happens, negative thoughts often pop up, such as, "I am climbing badly, I can't do this, or I'm about to fall." These types of thoughts put you in the negative mindset. The underlying feeling is that the climb will only be successful if you make perfect moves from start to finish, without making a mistake anywhere. Other climbers believe that if they are not super strong that they have no chance of doing a route with a grade of high difficulty. These are common assumptions about the conditions for success, which can become a self-fulfilling prophecy.'

What happens is that climbers no longer believe in themselves and then they focus more on the stress signals that their body is sending out, coupled with more associative, negative thoughts, until they no longer have a chance of success. 'I call it the 'red-flag' situation - this happens of course not only in climbing, but in other parts of our lives. You want to achieve something but it threatens to not work out. The red flag could be different things: it could be fear, it could be fatigue, it could be confusion, it could be anxiety, or something else that means you are no longer productive in reaching your goal.'

Hill regularly finds herself in a red-flag situation – both in her climbing life and outside of it. And what she does in such moments is as follows: stop, accept, re-group, and then continue.

Lynn explains how she employs 'stop', which is step one of her method: 'If I notice that my body is sending out stress signals, for example because I have ensnared myself with negative thoughts or doubt if I can do something, I force myself to take a pause and go over what the problem actually is, so I can make the correct decision about the challenge that I see in front of me. Before attempting a climb, I look for places where I can rest - a section of the rock where I can "shake out" the fatigue in my arms or legs and plan the next sequence of moves. In my daily life I simply go and sit somewhere or go for a walk with my dog, which allows me the time to think over what the problem is and how I can deal with it.'

ACCEPT

The thinking pause gives Hill the chance to make a distinction between objective circumstances (a foot that slipped, arm muscles that are cramping or other physical stress signals) and the feeling of uncertainty that arises through them (the fear or conviction that it is no longer possible to reach the top of the rock). The first is an objective fact, but the second is a subjective belief that does not have to be true. Once this clear distinction is made, step two of the method comes into play: acceptance.

'I recognize that I find myself in a difficult situation, that I'm tired, shocked by a slip and far from reaching my goal, and because of that I'm frightened or uncertain. I accept this feeling without resistance – so I don't think: "I don't wanna feel like this", but simply accept this is how I feel.'

However: in this acceptance phase, Hill does not allow herself to be overwhelmed by the idea that her goal has become unreachable, but just accepts the fact that she is beginning to *think* that because of the stress signals her body is sending out.

'If I have slipped, I think: "ok, my foot slipped - I'm about to fall!", which has happened, perhaps because I felt scared or doubted myself. But if I'm still hanging on, I still have a chance to make it all the way to the top. I don't turn a minor slip into a big story of failure, but I try to keep true to the factual observations. I remind myself that what happened was just a small mishap, nearly as insignificant as a fly landing on my shoulder.'

'And if I feel that my arms are becoming tired during the climb, I try not to believe the thought: "Oh no, my arms are getting tired and now I'm definitely going to fall", but I accept that I'm tired and that this state makes me scared of falling. I know that this signal from my body doesn't mean that I'm actually going to fall. I can still safely reach the top, as long as I take account of the fact that my arm muscles are quite tired and I will need to make sure to rest whenever possible by taking deep breaths of air and shaking out each arm one at a time. I try to anticipate the next rest point on my route so that I can relax my forearms and rest before running out of strength.'

REFRESH

With this new, positive thinking, Hill 'refreshes' her mind, as it were, and with a clear mind it is easier for her to perform well. She uses the same strategy during a climb if she starts doubting herself. 'If, on a climb, I realize that I am confused about where I have to go and how I can get past a difficult point, I look for a place to rest. Maybe I can't see what to do because I am really not able to find a good way to get up the rock, or perhaps I am so overcome by the challenge I'm facing that I've got tunnel vision? In the first case I can use this pause to properly consider what to do – perhaps I can now see the solution.'

In the second case – the tunnel vision – Hill first acknowledges her own uncertainty, and then tries to broaden her view. 'I look calmly around me, and look more broadly to each side, or higher than I had done until that point. Possibly I can suddenly see a solution to my problem just ahead of me. Perhaps I can climb more on the right side of the wall, if the left side is not doable. Perhaps I can shuffle my foot, and stand with my legs further apart. I try to look for things that I haven't tried yet and that could get me out of this difficult situation. What I certainly don't do is to keep on climbing while I still have no idea about my next step, or I'm filled with doubt – then it's definitely not going to work.'

Hill admits that her method can be time-consuming for people trying it for the first time, but she also has comforting news: the more often you practice, the quicker it becomes. 'I have been climbing for more than forty years, and for me this type of analysis has become intuitive. Nowadays I automatically use the strategy of stopping and mentally refreshing; I don't have to think consciously about doing it.'

LESSONS IN CLIMBING

It was different at the start of her climbing career, Hill recounts. 'I had to develop this method because I have climbed so many different places in the world. In every region I had to get used to a new type of rock, and with it another style of climbing. This means new doubts, problems and fears that I had to overcome. Each climb is its own little lesson, and through all the experiences I learned that most challenges can be overcome, as long as you employ the strategy of stopping, accepting and refreshing your mind before you keep going.'

Hill learned to climb as a teenager in California, on slabs and cracks, and low-angled faces. To climb these the main thing was to keep her balance, and put her feet firmly on the tiny protrusions on the wall. That taught her to make precise movements, and to check if she remained well-balanced during all her movements. Later on, Hill learned to climb steeper walls, walls that overhang, or rock formations made from stalactites and other gaps where you can put your fingers. 'That meant that I had to learn an unfamiliar climbing style. At the start I found it very difficult, and sometimes had the feeling that I was stuck, but I realized that, if you're small like me, the best thing is to align yourself so you can get a hold of something and get back into a good position, before continuing climbing. I also learned to make other dynamic moves, such as jumping up.'

Hill talks with great passion about climbing. While speaking, she makes movements that she would make on a wall; she raises her arms high above her head, and bends her knees and pushes them flat against her chest. Yet several times in our conversation she says that climbing is no longer the most important thing in her life. At the moment she is facing other challenges: she is bringing up her son, writing an autobiography, and making an educational video about the techniques and mechanics of climbing movement. But in the face of these challenges, she also regularly employs her method of 'stop, accept, refresh and continue'.

'These days I don't have any big climbing goals. I need my energy for other tasks in my life. But climbing has given me a number of skills that I still use in various situations where I want to perform well. The same skills that help me in difficult climbing situations can also help me solve problems in life. By pausing during moments of difficulty, and asking myself the right questions I am better able to find the right solutions; I am constantly analyzing problems, and identifying which aspects are not working as well as they could so that I can optimize and improve. First I must ask, "What is not working efficiently? What is stopping me from working productively? How can I solve this? Whatever challenge I come up against in my life, it has become second nature for me to observe the situation from an objective perspective, without judgement. That is a natural extension to what I do when I climb. I have trained myself in seeing things how they are. Not colored by how I want them to be, but how they actually are. This helps me focus on making things better and finding a solution.'

DISORDER

Climbing taught Hill to be observant about feelings that could negatively influence her performance. Previously, on the rocks, these were mostly feelings of uncertainty, caused by tiredness. These days, she is more often bothered by feelings of annoyance caused by distractions and disorder in her workspace environment.

'In recent years I have discovered that I function best in a clean and tidy environment. If I have to finish some important work, I don't like having excessive amounts of paperwork around me. They distract me, which makes me feel irritated and unsettled. First I accept what the problem is: I feel uncomfortable because of the disorder around me, then I take care of the mess before work.'

It is not always easy to see things as they are, says Hill, 'because this implies that you have to take action, to spend time, to properly deal with the observed problem. Many people don't want to do this. They don't want to tidy up their papers first, or to think deeply about what is really preventing them from achieving their goals. But it does not do us any good to hide things away or "sweep things under the rug", because they come out sooner or later and could have more serious negative results. So it is helpful to be critical and honest in daily life, and face problems or issues as they are, even though it is not always easy. Only by doing that can you progress and optimize your full potential in life.'

CHAPTER 13

MARTIN FICKWEILER

'DARE TO TAKE UNTRODDEN PATHS'

Martin Fickweiler (1977) is a Dutch mountaineer and big wall climber. But unlike many of his climbing colleagues, Fickweiler is not attracted to the world's most iconic walls. He prefers rock faces that have never been climbed before, and to hike through desolate mountainous areas where nature has remained pure.

He has always been wayward. When he was fifteen years old, someone once showed him a catalogue with photographs of climbers. Young Fickweiler decided that he wanted to climb, too, but he had no money or possibilities to travel to the mountains. And so he practiced by climbing public works of art and bridges in his neighborhood. When a climbing gym with a 115-feet high wall was built one-hour's cycle ride away, Martin knew he could now start practicing more seriously. He preferred climbing in the gym when no one else was there; at night, or when the weather outside was so bad hardly anyone felt like leaving their house. He didn't mind, he says: 'Often, when my parents thought I had packed my bag for school, I would take the bus to the gym; inside my bag was my climbing gear.'

UNDISCOVERED CLIMBS

When he grew older, he continued to be drawn to quiet, undiscovered areas. He climbed routes in Arctic Canada that had not been climbed before, as well as untouched routes in the Algerian Sahara, and in Greenland. Fickweiler explains that he feels drawn to such untrodden areas because he cannot anticipate what to expect from them. There are no climbers' stories about them that can help him, so he has to do it all by himself. To others, that might be scary, but Fickweiler loves this way of travelling and climbing. 'It makes that you really start to live in the present moment,' he says. 'There are no sounds of cars and roads in the background, you are not comparing your own experience to that of others – because there are none. All that remains is your own concentration on the climbing. During a long route, you will hike and climb, rest and eat – and you do everything in a state of concentration. Maintaining a deep focus can be really hard for me in my daily life in the Netherlands, because there, I am always occupied with a variety of different things at once. But during my climbs I easily reach that state of deep concentration. My life in the mountains is simple.'

Within the climbers' community, Fickweiler is known for his love for the unknown. Other climbers describe him as a man with a strong will, someone who dares to set goals that are interesting yet complex.

He mostly travels with only a small team of expedition members; he is not a guy for large groups. And his last big climbing trip, to Baffin Island in 2010, he made all by himself. For three weeks, he hiked, climbed and camped in the rough, cold landscape. A big challenge – both physically and mentally. Physically because, if something went wrong along the way, emergency assistance would not be near. And mentally because Fickweiler had known his whole life that he did not like being alone. Yet he wanted to test that conviction, and for that, he had to travel to one of the quietest places in the world.

'I used to think of myself as a joiner, someone who needed people around him in order to feel good. And this idea of myself was reflected in the practice of my daily life. I was never alone for longer than a few hours. Never. And I enjoyed that social lifestyle, but at the same time, it frightened me that I seemed to need others to feel happy and enjoy myself. A longing grew inside of me: I wanted to investigate what I would do if I were really alone.'

LURKING FEAR

Fickweiler started his investigation in the huge rocks of Yosemite Valley, In California. He climbed the full 2,953 feet alone, by self-belaying himself onto the rock. 'I selected a route called 'Lurking Fear' for my first big wall-solo climb. I had climbed on that rock six times before, but always with other climbers. You talk while you climb, you rest and eat together and you make bad jokes. I was high and away from the inhabited world, but never lonely. This time, I would be alone on the wall for three days. I wanted to know how that would feel.'

But he did not find the loneliness he was so curious about. Far away from the valley, he could still see the inhabited world from his portaledge. Far below him, he saw cars driving.

While he was resting or climbing, he could hear the voices of other climbers, below or above him on the rocks. And right before he had started his ascent, he had met tens of other climbers in the basecamp, and he knew that he would meet them and other climbers once he had finished his climb. Yosemite was packed with people. So while his first solo succeeded in the sense that he got to the top, it wasn't enough for him. He wanted more.

He cannot recall precisely when the idea took shape to travel to Baffin Island in Canada by himself, but it must have been shortly after he got home from Yosemite. It started as a vague plan, but soon transformed into a strong, compelling dream. And at some point, it seemed there was no other option: he just had to do it.

'I had been there twice before in my life, during expeditions with other climbers. Both times had been spectacular. The natural surroundings are amazing there, and I can really relate to the Inuit culture. Those people are still in close contact with the environment, they hunt animals to eat the flesh and use their skins to keep warm, they don't waste anything. I knew that Baffin Island has a lot of rocks that have never been climbed. That means that you can't be certain what to expect before you go on a trip there, you just have to trust your own climbing techniques and go for it. And, being in an area that is hardly ever visited by people, you find yourself far away from society. Both of the times I was climbing in Baffin Island, I felt far away from my daily life in the Netherlands.'

But he was never far away from his fellow climbers. He saw them ploughing through the snow, he heard them talking, and he shared freeze-dried meals with them. That would be different this time. This time, Fickweiler wanted to go to Baffin Island all alone, and he wanted to climb something that had never been climbed before. He looked on maps and selected a route for himself, estimated that he would need four or five weeks to hike and to climb it. He was ready for the loneliest experience of his life.

DOUBT

'When I made up that plan in my living room, it seemed awesome – I felt certain that I wanted to test myself, find out what loneliness would do to me. But as the time of departure neared, I became more and more nervous. I was thirty-three years old at that time, and I had participated in over twenty-five expeditions, so I was a very experienced climber. But now I started doubting whether I should pursue this plan, to go all by myself. I was in doubt when I booked my tickets. I was in doubt when I packed my bag. I was still in doubt when I kissed my girlfriend goodbye.'

The feeling of uncertainty grew after his airplane had landed in Canada, and Fickweiler had to transfer to a helicopter. He looked outside the window and noticed that his body felt tight from anxiety. While he felt utterly insecure at that point, it was not enough to make him turn around and go home. In his mind, he started to sum up arguments that would persuade him to pursue his plan. This area is so beautiful, he told himself, and he had selected a period in time when the sun in Baffin Island would not set – that was a good thing, it would make it more easy to hike and climb. Around him, he discovered remarkable rocks and ice-sheets, and he tried to focus his full attention on them, so that doubt could not dominate his mind.

So far so good – but in the village where the helicopter dropped him with his luggage, Fickweiler got some bad news. When he was making his plan, he had imagined that the Inuit could drop him off at the starting point of his route, then come and get him again at the end point. But when he asked them, they told him it was impossible, as that part of Baffin Island's ice was in bad condition, and they could not reach it with snow scooters.

By now, the doubt was raging through Fickweiler's body. This had to be a bad sign. He decided to stay put in the village for a couple of days to think, and eventually, he decided to adjust his plan. He would start at the same point he had had in mind for the initial plan, but then do a climb that seemed less hard, so that he would save enough energy to walk back all the way to the village – a hike of ninety-three miles that would take him ten days.

'After I had made my decision to continue with an adjusted plan, I still felt nervous. I remember waking up the morning of my departure with a sick stomach.' But he tried to ignore it as much as possible, and got on the back of a snow scooter. His wish to investigate a new part of the world and of his own identity was stronger than his doubt. He left his heavy gear behind in the village and took only his light gear – enough for the shorter trip he was now planning to make.

POLAR BEARS

His anxiousness increased on the snow scooter until it became almost unbearable, and then, suddenly, after the Inuit had dropped him off, it disappeared. 'I was in the middle of nowhere and I saw them driving away from me,' he recalls. 'And I became completely calm. I felt very clearly: I can do this, I am doing the right thing, And I started to walk.'

The advice he had received from the Inuit in the village helped him during his trip. For example, about how to move most safely and efficiently among the polar bears living in the area. 'Live like they live', the Inuit had told him, 'do what they do'. When they told him that, Fickweiler had nodded politely without truly understanding the meaning of the words, but now he started to get what they meant. 'Polar bears are active at night and sleep during the day,' he said. 'I had to make that rhythm my own: walking during the night and sleeping during the day. It made it easier to walk because, at night, the ice would become hard and I would not sink in as much. And the sunlight would have warmed up the air by the time I was ready for bed. Besides, this rhythm allowed me a peaceful sleep – I did not have to fear hunting polar bears.'

His first night in his tent, he indeed slept deeply and peacefully. The only thing that disturbed him a few times was the self-made polar bear alarm he had made out of two ski poles and a string with tiny bells. It had been his own idea: he figured that if a polar bear touched the tent, he would be alerted by the sound of clinging bells. The problem was that the wind constantly set off the alarm. The next night, he decided to sleep without an alarm. He was sure the polar bears would leave him alone. After all, the Inuit should know.

And he started to trust in himself, more and more.

He started to learn what he needed to do in order to keep functioning in the extreme circumstances of the Arctic. He followed a strict regime of hiking, eating and sleeping at certain times. He would hike for some hours, pitch his tent, cook a big portion of freeze dried food, eat half and keep the other half in a Tupperware box for the next day. Then he would set his alarm, sleep, have breakfast, and start hiking again.

DIARY

He lived like this for three weeks. No one around him, a constant view of snow and ice. And while, for all those years, he had feared that he would find it extremely hard to be isolated from other human beings, now he discovered he did not mind being alone at all. He didn't even feel lonely, was completely absorbed by his daily schedule and activities. Hiking, finding the right way to go. Preparing for the night, preparing food. He did talk to himself out loud, Fickweiler admits to me – perhaps because that gave him a sense of companionship, or perhaps just something to do. 'I had taken a video camera with me, and every day I would record myself, making a daily diary. It was a nice thing to do during the trip, to be able to speak about how I was feeling and what I was seeing when I looked around me, but I never looked at the film clips afterwards.'

Fickweiler also carried a satellite phone with him, in case of emergencies. 'Luckily, I stayed safe and healthy during my trip, but just the idea of having the option to ask for assistance gave me some peace of mind. Maybe, if I were to do this trip again, I would not take the satellite phone with me. I think that might complete the sense of isolation, of being alone. But even with the phone in my bag, I felt further away from my normal life than I had ever been, and closer to nature. I am very much aware that that idea is not completely fair, because I was wearing warm shoes and clothing that I had bought in specialized, expensive shops that one finds in the modern world. But still – there I was, surrounded by nature, and no other human beings around me. I found that surprisingly nice. I was actually kind of sad when my trip was ending.'

Although the trip itself went much easier than he had expected, it proved harder than expected to fit back into his old life, in the Netherlands.

His time on Baffin Island had changed him in a way that he did not see coming beforehand. He had liked it so much being alone, that he now longed to be alone more often. Back home, he had difficulties picking up his usual social life. 'All I wanted was to sit in my little boat by myself and sail,' he tells me. 'Or I wanted to go climbing – again, by myself. Those were the only things that made me happy, and it seemed like I couldn't find the energy to do anything else. But it was impossible for me to live like that. I had a girlfriend – she is now my wife – and you just can't be that egocentric once you're in a relationship. So the period after my return from Baffin Island was a very difficult period for the both of us. Luckily, my extreme longing to be alone decreased over time.'

SILENCE

Later he noticed that his trip had changed yet another thing about him. It was as if the silence that he had experienced on Baffin Island, had travelled back with him to the Netherlands. He did not have to embark on another journey to feel at ease. That feeling of calm and ease had become a permanent state of being.

'Until I had challenged myself on Baffin Island, my whole life was about planning new expeditions', he says. 'Travelling back from one expedition, I would already start planning a new one. As soon as I read about an untrodden area in a magazine, I wanted to go there, the sooner the better. I had the same response when I heard other climbers talking about their adventures. Clearly, there was a lot of restlessness within me. I was driven towards new climbing trips, all the time. You could say that I was trying to flee from the normal world, and that I was using extreme climbing projects to distract myself from my own discomfort. I felt happy and calm only in areas where the environment was quiet, and the view steep and airy.'

But after Baffin Island, Fickweiler noticed that he did not feel drawn to do yet another trip. Instead, he noticed he was tired. Not just physically, but more so mentally. Tired of travelling, Tired of living as a climber. Tired of travelling, having to carry heavy gear, the flying, the coordinating and planning of his trips. He was done, he says: 'As if this lonely experience had taught me that I was enough. Maybe I had expected that this first solo expedition would be the start of many others, but in reality, that was not the case at all. It was the end of my big wall expeditions. I've proven myself enough.'

At the moment of writing this book, Fickweiler has a son of six years old, and he works as a photographer of climbing areas and climbers. He has not made any more extreme alpine tours, or other big trips since he returned from Baffin Island. But he still finds ways to be alone, he tells me: 'I go to the climbing gym quite often by myself, preferably one with an outdoor-wall. I self-belay, and climb up and down. I don't hear anything, don't think of anything, I just concentrate fully on how I place my feet on the holds, my breathing. Deeply inhaling and exhaling. The sound of my breath creates a rhythm, a back noise that calms me, even if the climbing becomes a little frightening, say, if I am climbing right above a piece of rock that could hurt me if I fell.'

Fickweiler underlines that climbers have to be able to trust themselves, fully. 'And thanks to my journeys, and especially my solo expedition, I know I can completely trust myself. I know that it might take me longer or shorter than I had expected, the route can be more difficult or easier, but whatever happens, I will always survive, as long as I stay concentrated, act in a rhythm, and do not give up. As long as I stick to those rules, I will always be fine.'

CHAPTER 14

STEPH DAVIS

'EXPECT THE UNEXPECTED'

Americans rock climber, BASE jumper and wingsuit flyer Steph Davis (44) understands the risks of her sports, perhaps more than anyone. In 2013, on their summer visit to the Italian Dolomites, her husband Mario Richard died after flying off a mountain in a wingsuit. Davis had jumped from the same spot, seconds before him. She flew through the air and had a safe landing. But her husband impacted the rock, and did not survive.

It may seem incomprehensible that, confronted with so much evidence for the risk inherent to her sports, Davis continues to BASE jump and wingsuit. But she jumps off rocks in her wingsuit regularly at home in Moab Utah, as well as around the US and Europe, and almost always together with her current partner Ian. And, to top that, she feels more present and grateful than ever before – she says she has never been so happy in her life.

'Losing Mario devastated me, but through the journey of grief and acceptance I have learned a lot about happiness and gratitude. Life is about the journey, and about how we choose to experience it. Happiness is the way. I have also learned that you can try and plan everything in life – whether it is a relationship, or an athletic endeavor, or some aspect of your future – but life will always unfold in unexpected ways. I now know that in any unexpected situation, I will find a way to get through it. I know that I can count on myself, no matter what happens.'

Chapter 14 - Steph Davis

HOOKED

Let's go back to a point earlier in Davis' story. As a freshman at university, she was invited by a classmate to join him for a day of rock climbing. That first time on the rocks would change her life forever. After earning a Master's degree in literature and then starting law school, she decided to leave academia and climb full time. Climbing, she felt, could offer her everything that she needed and loved in life. Living outside in nature, challenging herself, practicing movement for hours in complete concentration...Davis was hooked.

Steph Davis was quickly becoming one of the best female climbers in the world. She made first ascents in Pakistan, Baffin Island and Kyrgyzstan. She was the only woman who ever free solo climbed a route with difficulty rating 5.11+ (6c, in the French climbing grades) without using a rope or other safety gear, and she became the second woman to free climb El Capitan in a day (Lynn Hill was the first; her memories are captured in chapter 12). She became the first woman to free climb the Salathe Wall on El Capitan. Davis was the first woman to ever climb the famous peak Torre Egger in Patagonia, as well as the seven peaks of the Fitzroy Range in Argentina. She made four historic free solo climbs of the Longs Peak Diamond in Colorado, a high altitude big wall, climbing with no rope.

But after a difficult split from her first husband Dean Potter in 2007, Davis looked for a departure from her normal life and plunged into skydiving. Within a few months, she had learned to fly wingsuits and to BASE jump, and then started to practice the most extreme form of these sports: wingsuit BASE jumping. It was through jumping that she met her future husband Mario Richard, while he was flying the skydiving plane in Moab, Utah.

CONTROL

A new phase in her life had started, balancing both climbing and flying and working to keep herself at a high level in both. Davis became a pioneer in combining climbing with BASE jumping, making several BASE climbs from rock towers in Moab, Utah, and a wingsuit BASE climb from Notch Peak, the second tallest vertical cliff face in the US (after El Cap), while continuing to pursue difficult free ascents of desert cracks. She explains that to her BASE jumping is a physical expression of both personal responsibility and freedom. 'Humans have always dreamed of flight,' she says.

'BASE jumping has brought me some of the greatest joy in my life, and it has also brought me the most pain. As Mario always said, "everything has to balance". Jumping is in many ways much more mental and emotional than it is physical, and it forces you to work beside your fear rather than trying to hide from it or eliminate it.' Davis manages her fear by using two seemingly paradoxical methods that she has developed in recent years: on the one hand, she prepares in detail for each and every jump that she makes and, on the other hand, she believes that BASE jumping, as much as any mountain sport, is an activity that cannot be totally planned and prepared for, and consciously expects the unexpected.

'I prefer to do things when I know I'm truly prepared, often beyond prepared, because I really want to be very present through the whole experience, rather than distracted by doubt. That experience of presence is what I'm really looking for.'

In contrast, playing with destiny is *not* the type of experience that Davis is after in her sports. 'I try to prepare as well as I can for each jump. I make sure to know the metrics of the site, I evaluate the wind, and I analyze the flight line in detail. I make sure there are "outs"—different lines to take if my original plan isn't working. I train a lot through skydiving and frequent BASE jumping. It's also important to be very fit, so that you arrive at the top feeling fresh instead of exhausted – you have to carry your gear to the top of the cliff or mountain, and if you're tired, it's difficult to focus.'

REFLECTING ON FEARS

Another way to prepare for both jumping and climbing is to reflect on her own fears: learning to understand how fear impacts her body movement and concentration is crucial, she says. 'We get very affected by fear in our sports. So figuring out how to work with fear, rather than getting completely controlled by it, is important. The feeling of fear is often more about anxiety of what *might* happen, rather than what actually is happening. So trying to figure out how to not be so affected by emotions is very important. Allowing yourself to be controlled physically by fear can actually be more dangerous than the activity you're trying to do.'

As part of the pre-jump analysis, she visualizes the moment of leaving the edge, the flight she will make, deploying the parachute, and then landing. She also visualizes her plan B and C, what she will do if things change unexpectedly. 'Only then do I make the decision to jump, or not. If the conditions don't feel right—too much wind, too many clouds—or if I am just not feeling it for any reason, I turn around and walk down. Sometimes, it just doesn't feel right. If there's anything I don't like, I always make the decision to not jump.'

Davis is clearly aware that BASE jumping involves many risks that are beyond her control. 'It is always possible that something will happen that you could not have prepared for. The wind can pick up unexpectedly, or the air or the weather can change after you jump. Air is invisible, so it's difficult for us to gauge it perfectly. And the reality of being in the mountains is that you simply can't predict everything.'

When I ask whether she has now become free of fear, after so many years of practice, she bursts out laughing: 'Absolutely not. The point is not to not be afraid. I think that if you choose to enter dynamic environments, it's important to have an understanding of the danger. You also have to be able to objectively evaluate why it is dangerous. And then the question is, how do you operate when you truly understand everything that can happen? The difference is between feeling fear versus being controlled by fear. So I feel it all the time, but I have been practicing controlling myself in the presence of fear, for all these years. And this helps me a lot with the rest of my life as well.'

MARIO RICHARD

Her husband Mario Richard understood this deeply, she feels. He was very focused on safety but he was never controlled by fear. He was also an expert BASE jumper. When Davis and Richard met, he had been skydiving for almost thirty years and BASE jumping for over twenty, and was known as a pioneer of the sport. He understood the risks that are part of the sport, and took them extremely seriously. He was a pilot, a parachute rigger, had built his own gear, and had made thousands of jumps around the world.

Richards and Davis were jumping from the Sass Pordoi in Italy. They had jumped from the mountain twice the day before and returned the next morning, enjoying the perfect weather. As usual, he let her go first and kissed her goodbye. Davis focused her attention, took a deep breath, launched from mountain and flew. After she had landed safely on the ground, she waited for her husband to land behind her. But he never arrived. Davis would later learn that after he followed her off the edge, he had impacted just a few meters too low while flying over a notch in the rock, the same path he'd flown twice safely the day before.

After fatal BASE jump accidents, it is always hard to track down what precisely went wrong. So it will remain forever a mystery why an experienced and careful jumper like Richard would have an accident during his flight, especially as the conditions were perfect and he'd flown the same line without incident the day before. Richard had switched to contacts from glasses right before the trip, and he had been having trouble with the contact lenses the day before, and Davis now suspects his vision may have been compromised, more than he realized—for her, it's the only explanation of an extremely inexplicable accident. Losing her husband left her emotionally shattered. Back at home in Moab, she used climbing and short BASE jumps as a way to get herself out of the house, to keep herself from going into a deep depression. But she felt unsure that she would fly wingsuits again because the joy of flight was now connected to the ultimate loss. After several months had passed, she decided that hiding from pain was not the answer. She had to find the courage to fly again, to see if the joy was still there.

LIBERATING

The first jump that Davis made after the death of her husband was 'extremely, extremely intense. It was very difficult not to let my mind go back to our last jump, to the last time I saw Mario. In order to fly safely, you have to be able to control your emotions, and obviously it was hard for me to push them out while standing at the edge of a cliff in my wingsuit, this time without Mario behind me, when the last time I flew I'd lost everything. But as soon as I left the edge, it all came back, the joy as well as the pain. I felt him in the air and when I touched the ground, I cried. I knew I had to go on living and go on flying. It's a part of me, and it was a part of us. When I'm in the air, I feel close to Mario, because he really lived in the air and to me, that's where he is now. Through this journey I've come to understand that everything is uncertain. When we imagine we know what our future will be like, in reality, we have no clue. Life can change in a second, and it does. This can be a scary thought, but it's actually comforting: change is the one thing you can be sure of in life. The only thing you can control is yourself. Beyond that, the only option that you have, really, is to embrace uncertainty and let go. Life is change.'

Davis believes that while we can't control things that happen, we always control how we feel. And choosing joy is the way she honors Mario's memory.

'When Mario died, I felt completely hopeless. I didn't see the point of living at first. Over time I realized that it's up to us to decide how much happiness we have in life. Mario loved the air and he loved life. What made him happiest was bringing happiness to others. During the grief period, I realized I had two choices: not live, or truly live. I decided to live, to really live, and to choose joy.'

Her experiences have made her much better able to embrace uncertainty, Davis explains. 'There are many things we believe or aspire to, but until we actually live through an experience we can't fully understand it. I've always believed in the idea of joy at sudden disappointment, but that requires a lot of faith. When I was younger, I struggled with believing in myself and with self-confidence; now, I know that I can handle anything that happens. The real meaning of resilience is not just enduring through loss, but emerging from the dark times as a stronger, more grateful person. And this is the meaning of joy at sudden disappointment: being thankful for everything that comes. I'm thankful I had Mario in my life. The pain of losing him was worth the gift of knowing him.'

Davis climbs, jumps and flies most days. 'I love the mountains and I love the air. Like climbing, flying is part of my life, part of the way I experience the world. I prepare as well as I can for the risks I can predict, and realize at the same time that I will never be able to prepare completely for whatever might come next. Ultimately, life isn't about trying to hide from every possible risk. It's about opening your arms and embracing magic, about choosing to fly.'

CHAPTER 15

REBECCA WILLIAMS

'PRACTICE MINDFULNESS'

Rebecca Williams is a British climber, clinical psychologist and climbing coach. She combines scientific knowledge about anxiety performance with practical training for mountaineers and sport climbers. She tries to help climbers who underperform due to a mental barrier by teaching them cognitive behavioral skills, mindfulness practices and relaxation exercises, such as self-hypnosis.

She emphasizes that all the techniques that she teaches her clients are scientifically proven effective. They have helped tens of climbers who were so afraid to fall that they did not dare to select challenging projects for themselves, or did not reach their goals despite training hard. Nevertheless, Williams' methods are not widely known and used in the climbing world, she says. She sighs before she continues to speak: 'Fear is still a taboo among most climbers. People speak relatively little about it, and very few seriously train themselves to deal with fear. Climbers tend to train their muscles, rather than work on their performance anxiety or their fear of falling.'

Working on these issues offers great opportunities for improvement. 'Almost all climbers, at some point in their career, are confronted with feelings of fear. If you can't see their fear while they are climbing, that's probably because they are trying to hide it from outsiders. Sure, some climbers are more afraid than others, for example because they have vertigo, or perhaps because they are very perfectionistic, but there is only a very small minority that is never, ever afraid. And we all know that fear has a negative impact on performance, so that means that if athletes want to become better, they will have to face their fears.'

TABOO

Williams has asked many of the climbers she has met over the years why they think that fear remains a taboo topic in the climbing sector, and she has distilled several reasons from their answers. 'Many think that it has to do with peer pressure, or what psychologists call negative social evaluation,' she says. 'Like all human beings, climbers want to be accepted in the group, and therefore admitting that you are more afraid than someone else becomes scary in itself – it threatens your membership of that group.

A second reason for the fear taboo is that many people find it complicated to deal with complex emotions like their fears, especially as adults. We want to be competent, we want to be good at what we do. Fear reminds us that things do not work out the way we had planned, and that we can fail. That's an uncomfortable idea for many people. In order not to be confronted with that uncomfortable feeling, we tend to avoid fear-inducing situations – for example by only selecting climbing routes that are easy for us, so that we know for sure we won't fail.' For similar reasons, many climbers do not even like to talk about their fearful experiences, as that would only remind them of their own frailties.

And Williams offers a third explanation for the fear taboo: the image of climbers. 'The wider public still holds this perception that climbers are daredevils. This is also the picture you get from films and other media: there, mountaineers are portrayed as sensation-seekers, exceptionally brave, or perhaps even a bit crazy, because they want to do such scary things. But in reality, those representations don't resemble the personality characteristics of climbers at all. Research shows that most climbers are careful, thoughtful types, and that they dislike taking big risks or giving away control. Plus, they are often very perfectionistic: they hate it when they are not good at what they do.' With such strong stereotypes at play, many climbers try to hide their fear and doubts from each other and the outside world.

Williams hopes that the topic of fear will be approached with less negativity by climbers in the nearby future. She is convinced that the desire to overcome fear is the main reason why so many people are attracted to the sport, and that it is the continual struggle with fear that makes the sport so interesting. 'Learning to overcome the fear that rises as soon as you go high up can give you an enormous sense of power,' she says. 'It offers you proof that, even in anxious situations, you are able to stay in control. That you can push yourself to a great performance, despite your fear. Imagine a climber who starts to feel afraid halfway up her route, but decides to continue to ascend and succeeds in controlling her fear and moving forward, concentrated and undisturbed by her fear. Can you imagine how proud and self-assured that climber will feel when she stands on the top? She has conquered her own emotions. And her performance may have been less impressive if she had climbed without ever being bothered by fear.'

MINDFUL

But how about athletes who are not able to overcome their fears, I ask, and who underperform as a result? 'There's a couple of very effective methods that help you to cope with fears, that everyone can learn,' Williams replies. 'They're not just useful for climbers, but for everyone who wants to reach a certain goal and feels hampered by fears. Someone who wants to give a public lecture but is bothered with stage fright, for example – maybe he is so afraid that he can no longer remember what he wanted to say as soon as he climbs up onto that stage. Or someone who is given a complicated task at work, but is afraid he is not experienced or smart enough to do it. Maybe that fear means he does not dare to make any decisions by himself, which slows down the project. There are relatively easy methods in all such common situations that can help you calm down, so that the tension will no longer stop you from performing at your best.'

The first method that she describes indeed seems simple: observing whether there are negative thoughts crossing your mind when you are about to perform, like "I can't do this", or "I will blow this". If you notice any, you should lead your attention away from such thoughts and concentrate on your body. For example, focusing on your seat bones pressing into the chair you're sitting on, or on the rising and falling of your stomach as you breathe. Somewhat surprisingly, this mindfulness technique is still little used by sports coaches. 'Observing negative thoughts is something that almost all psychologists advise to insecure or underperforming clients – that has become common practice. But usually, the client is then advised to regard those thoughts critically and counter-pose them with positive thoughts, like "I can do this, I will succeed".'

Williams found that this rational method is rather ineffective for most people. 'They try to think positively as best as they can and they come up with beautiful affirmations, but they don't really believe in them, and therefore they don't work. Another reason why this method is often ineffective is that if we focus our attention on thoughts – even if it is to come up with counter arguments – we make them larger and more important in our minds.'

That is why Williams recommends an alternative – mindfulness – as an approach to negative thinking. 'Don't focus on the negative thoughts that you have observed in your mind, but focus on the body. Feel what your hands are doing while you are placing the paper with the text you are going to read on stage in front of you. Notice how your feet are standing on the stage, how your fingers are holding the microphone. If you concentrate really deeply on such physical experiences, you'll automatically distract your mind from concerns and doubts.'

In order to get the hang of this method, it's important to practice it often. Shifting your attention from thinking to sensing will not just calm you down, but it also helps you to become aware of how many judgments we make of ourselves and the situations we find ourselves in. Realizing how rigid we think about what we should be able to do helps us to become more compassionate with ourselves – and that takes away part of the tension. Williams explains how this method can be applied whenever we are faced with an activity that we find scary: 'As soon as you notice that you are doubting whether you are capable enough to do something, try to consider those thoughts as passing clouds in the sky. They'll come and go naturally. You don't have to go along with them, and you don't have to find counterarguments for them. You'll see that if you pay no attention to them, just observe them and re-shift your focus to your body, they'll disappear naturally.'

DEEP RELAXATION AND SELF-HYPNOSIS

A second technique that is useful for people dealing with performance anxiety is a form of self-hypnosis. It works like this: you start with a so-called body scan, a meditation exercise in which you scan through your whole body, as it were, and try to identify in which parts you feel physical tension. Next, you try to let go of the tension in those parts by consciously relaxing the muscles. So, for instance, if you've noticed that your shoulders are tense, you now let them drop. And if you've been clenching your teeth, you relax the muscles in your jaw. Step three of this method is to close your eyes, and count slowly from twenty down to one. Step four is to imagine yourself in a situation that you associate with complete relaxation. That may be sitting in a hot bath filled with bubbles, or hiking through a lovely, hilly area with spectacular views all around you. It doesn't matter what situation you think of, as long as it works for you and provides you with a happy and relaxed feeling. 'If you imagine yourself in that situation and you intensely concentrate on that image,' Williams says, 'you'll bring down the level of adrenaline in your body. You're calming yourself down. If you are able to do that right before starting a scary task, you'll concentrate better and be better able to act precisely. That will make it much easier to perform well.'

Williams explains that it is important to become familiar with this method by practicing, initially, in non-stressful situations. 'So don't start using this method for the first time right before making a public speech or during a sport competition. That's for later, after you've trained yourself in this practice and have learned what works best for you. Start by practicing at home, in bed or on the couch.'

Once you're able to lower your level of adrenaline in familiar and non-stressful circumstances, Williams recommends continuing to practice in situations that resemble the one that stresses you out, but which aren't yet the real deal. For climbers with a fear of falling, this might be the base of a rock that they want to climb in the nearby future. 'You promise yourself that you will not quite yet make an attempt, but you will put on your shoes and harness,' she says. 'Next, you do the meditation exercise. Once you feel calm, you climb a route that is easy and not scary to you.' Likewise, someone with stage fright can practice self-hypnosis in the room where she will at some point want to give a speech – but without an audience. 'Go to the meeting room or whatever space you want to get on stage, do the exercise, and then have a drink there or read the newspaper, answer some e-mails, read a book perhaps. That way, your body will learn to associate this feeling of calm with the space in which you find yourself.'

The more often you practice, the better, Williams emphasizes: 'This exercise teaches you how you can calm yourself down, and that is a skill in which you can get better and faster by doing it more often. Once you've became really good at it in non-stressful situations, it will become much more easy for you to apply it in situations in which you do feel afraid.'

REDUCING PRESSURE

A third method that Williams often recommends her clients, is reducing the pressure to perform, and increasing the fun. 'This is a really easy technique that can help in situations where you want to perform well, but you feel so tense that there seems no way even to start. Your heart pounds in your chest, your breathing is fast and shallow, you're shaking from nervousness. That will make it hard to reach your goal, for sure. What helps is to temporarily lower your expectations, so that the pressure to perform decreases. This gives you some time to relax your body, it allows you to actually enjoy what you are doing, and eventually, it will make it easier for you to succeed.'

An anxious climber should wait a little before she starts the difficult route that she has planned to do, and warm up on a couple of easy routes. Or, she could start a difficult route and then consciously make jokes with her belayer. Not trying to avoid mistakes or even to succeed – but allowing yourself to be clumsy, and laugh about it. 'You probably won't do a very good job, and that's fine, because the goal of this exercise was to put joy back into your sport, and that lowers the stress levels in your body.'

Wannabe public speakers could apply this method by practicing their speeches and making as many mistakes as they possibly can. Preferably, they should do so in front of a mirror or – if they dare – in front of a small group of friends. 'Forget your text,' Williams says. 'Stutter. Trip over your own feet when you walk on to the stage. Fall silent and look around you with a goofy face. Whatever you do: laugh at yourself. This helps to lower the level of adrenaline. Then, try again and do the same – make as many mistakes as you can think off, act so that everything that can go wrong goes wrong, then laugh about it and come up with a contingency plan for how you will deal with anything that goes wrong. The third time, try how it feels to give the speech without consciously making mistakes. But don't try to avoid mistakes, either. Keep an open mind and see what happens. If you make a mistake, laugh. If you notice you're doing well, that probably means you have been able to lower the stress levels in your body.'

Whether or not you intend to apply Williams' methods, do not in any case deny that you are afraid or uncertain, she warns. 'Everybody is sometimes bothered by such feelings, and they will impact on you negatively as long as you try to push them away or try not to feel them, or don't come up with a plan for how to manage them. They're there, and with a high adrenaline level in your body it will become hard to perform at your best.'

So instead, recognize feelings of fear, and work on managing them. 'If you start understanding and accepting that scared side of yourself, and if you start to know how you can quickly calm yourself, you will become able to perform at your best even in the scariest situations. Once you find out that a relaxation method of twenty minutes really helps you to feel calm, please grant yourself that before you start your public speech or whatever challenging performance awaits you. Do it, even if none of the other people around you are doing it. They may use different methods to help them to stay calm, or they may hide their fears from you. Don't copy that; do things your own way. To perform well, you don't necessarily need to be extremely talented, or brave, or strong. The main thing is to be able to stay relaxed and focused in stressful situations – and everyone can learn that.'

AFTERWORD

APPLYING THE METHODS OF EXTREME ATHLETES IN NOT-SO-EXTREME SITUATIONS

FIFTEEN DIFFERENT ATHLETES, each with their own approach to fear, and each with their own methods to cope with it. To some extent, their views and strategies are personal. They are the result of years or even decades of experimenting, practicing, not daring, still wanting, still not daring, then doing it anyway. For most of the athletes I interviewed for this book, this process has been one of continuous self-examination of their deepest fears and motivations; for others, understanding the impact of fear on their own performance seemed to develop from practice; just by doing and learning along the way, they eventually reached their highest goals.

If the methods are individual and personal, then it follows that what might work well for one may not make any sense for another. In fact, some of the tips presented in this book run directly counter to one another. Take, for example, mountaineer Edurne Pasaban: she recommends coping with fear by allowing your gut feeling to govern your decisions – even if that means that you will have to give up on your goal, at least temporarily. Ambition is a great thing, her story suggests, but your life and wellbeing are ultimately the most important. Her colleague Martin Fickweiler, however, hints that sometimes it is good to ignore those deep-rooted feelings of fear. Push through your boundaries and you might surprise yourself, he says. And what about highliner Alexander Schulz, who is able to retain his balance under great pressure by repeating positive affirmations and pushing aside all negative thoughts, while 'builderer' Dan Goodwin invites all negative scenarios to cross his mind before he starts an ascent?

Which advice will help you to deal with your particular fear depends, of course, on your individual character, the type of fear you are dealing with, and the situation you find yourself in. Readers of this book often tell me that they feel intuitively which of the methods directly resonate with them, and which seem 'not for them'. I understand that, but I'd also strongly encourage you to experiment with methods that may not speak to you initially – you don't know how well they might work until you try them out, and they might be just what you need to leap over that edge. So try them out, whenever you can. Reread the book – or the parts that speak to you right then and there – whenever you face a new challenge in life and are confronted with fear or self-doubt. Become familiar with a broader range of fear-coping strategies, then pick and choose which of them seem useful in whatever new, scary situation you find yourself in.

Despite of the fact that this book presents people's personal approaches and methods to fear, I came to realize while writing it that several overlapping factors can be distilled from all the stories. In other words: there seem to be a couple of universal strategies to cope with fear – strategies that are useful for most people who want something, but are afraid to go for it – and strategies that apply to a wide range of frightening situations.

WORK THAT FEAR

One aspect that recurred throughout the stories was the idea of 'working with your fear'. All of the athletes seemed to agree that there is no use in denying fear. Fear is a strong emotion that can have serious negative impacts on your performance – and those impacts will not go away if you act as if you are not afraid. Fear impacts your body – it makes your breath shallow, it tenses your muscles. Fear impacts your mind –

it produces a vicious circle of panicking thoughts, making it hard for you to act with precision and concentration. Sometimes, if you deny or ignore your fear, it will take up such a dominant place in your life that it will stand in the way of your personal growth. This is what happens to people who decide that they cannot do something even before they try it. If you want to stop fear from obstructing your growth in whatever sphere of your life, whether that is your personal development, work or sports, acknowledging it is the very first step you simply have to take.

ROOT FEARS

The next step is to investigate what exactly lies beneath the fear. This requires self-reflection, as the feeling of fear can sometimes be too undefined to target, or even downright misleading. Sometimes we think we are afraid to fall, while in reality we are afraid to fail in the eyes of others. Sometimes we think we are afraid to trust someone else while what we really fear is having to rely on ourselves. Overcoming each of these fears requires a different method. To know where your fear is coming from, one strategy that I personally find very useful is to ask yourself 'why' when you are confronted with a feeling of fear, and to keep asking that until you've come to the root of the problem. You can ask yourself the question out loud, or write it down, together with the answer that comes to you, in a notebook.

This exercise might look like this:

'I am afraid to make the wrong decision in quitting my job.'

'Why?'

'Because if I don't find another job soon, I will have no income.'

'And why is that scary?'

'Because then I can't pay the rent.'

'And why is that scary?'

'Because then I have no place to go and I would have to ask my parents for help.'

Afterword

'*And why is that scary?*'

'Because then my father is going to say that I am very irresponsible.'

'*And why is that scary?*'

'Because... he's always said that I am not organized enough and that my brother was better at organizing his life.'

Bingo – now we're getting somewhere. So in this example, the stress experienced is not caused by the fear of quitting a job as such; it has to do with the fear of being rejected by your loved ones. This might seem like a far-fetched example, but it's not really. I find that an astonishing amount of fears come down to social acceptance, and the very human fear of not being part of the group, or of not being good enough.

Another example, from the field of sports:

'I am so nervous about this upcoming competition.'

'*Why?*'

'Because I want to win and I'm afraid I won't.'

'*Why is that scary?*'

'Because this will be my one chance and I have worked really hard for it and it will be such a downer if I blow it.'

'*Why?*'

'Because my trainer has invested so much time in me and I have been on this training schedule that drives my girlfriend crazy and then it will all have been for nothing.'

'*And why is that scary?*'

'Because then they will be disappointed with me and they will think I don't have enough talent to keep doing this.'

Boom.

Getting the point? So, investigate the factors underlying the shallow feeling of fear, select an appropriate method to deal with those root fears, and then work that fear.

PREPARE

The third aspect that ran through all athletes' stories has to do with thorough preparation. What often may seem, to outsiders, spontaneous or reckless actions, have in fact been practiced and rehearsed in detail. Sometimes this involves practicing a scary move over and over again until the body has become so familiar with it that it can be done automatically, without hesitation or doubt. Sometimes it means visualizing or imagining the action, or collecting all the information needed for a certain plan and going through the scenarios of what might happen in minute detail. Whatever method is best suited to the athletes that I spoke to, all of them take their preparations extremely seriously, and it is because of these detailed preparations – not just their talent or their guts – that they are able to succeed again and again under highly challenging conditions.

CALMING BODY AND MIND

A fourth factor is being able to calm yourself quickly in moments of stress. Self-reflection and detailed preparations may be crucial in lessening feelings of fear, but they will not always be sufficient to make fear disappear completely. Being afraid is something that human beings cannot *not* be; it is like being curious, or hungry, or distracted by the things you see or hear around you. That is how our bodies and minds were set up; they're all part of the deal of being human. While it is impossible to not have these responses, it is possible to learn not to act upon them. To act, rather than react to these very human characteristics. You can choose not to ask for gossip even though you might be keen to know what happened; you can choose not to eat that chocolate even if you would like to; and you can decide to do something even though you are afraid of it. Moreover, you can teach yourself to perform at your best despite your fear.

The way to do that is to learn to recognize your body's physical stress responses and applying methods that can help you to decrease the amount of adrenaline and other stress hormones in your body. Deep and regular breathing is one popular method; making use of positive affirmations another. Several of the athletes apply mindfulness exercises that distract the mind away from negative thoughts and self-doubt and into the present moment, or practice various forms of meditation and self-hypnosis. The key is to get to understand your body and know what works for you; practicing calming methods in non-stressful situations first, then becoming able to use them in stressful situations as well.

PRACTICE BEING AFRAID

The final overlapping factor – and perhaps the most important one of all – is that, in order to perform well under stress, you need to practice being afraid on a regular basis. That means stepping outside of your comfort zone and into situations that you find slightly – or very – scary. They don't have to be dangerous situations – better not, in fact; you were just practicing, remember? – but they should be a little uncomfortable. For you, that may be at the meeting table at work, where you promise yourself that you will raise your hand and express your opinion at least once. Or it might be halfway up a wall, right before a committing move but safely tied into a rope. Or it might be when you're sitting next to your driving instructor, or during your first drawing class or your first time on a longboard (why not?).

Frequently doing things that are new and a little scary to you will help you to recognize stress responses that are typical for your body, and to apply methods to cope with that stress. If you do that often enough, you will become better able to keep up your performance in spite of fear creeping up.

BECOMING BRAVE(R)...

I guess the downside of these conclusions is that overcoming fear is not something you do once in your life and then never have to do again ("Me? Afraid? Oh, I *used to be* like that, too – but not anymore!"). Unfortunately, I found little evidence for that popular idea of shock therapy in the research on risk behavior and fear management – both for this book and for my other work on these themes. What became most clear from the athletes' narratives is that overcoming fears and dealing with nervousness or anxiety are skills that need to be developed, kept up and maintained for the rest of your life. If you don't practice them for too long, they will weaken, just as 'Spiderman' Alain Robert's vertigo pops up again if he hasn't climbed for a while.

The plus side of that, though, is that 'being brave' is not a fixed trait that you are born with – or not. Not at all – it is a characteristic that you can develop yourself. If you invest in it, you grow it – and you might be able to do things that you'd never thought you would ever dare to do.

The life histories of the athletes that I've woven through the chapters in this book show that these people were not born without fear. They, too, struggled with performance anxiety, or vertigo, or the fear of getting hurt. In that sense, they are just like you and me. What distinguishes them from most of us, though, is that they have learned to overcome their fears, and are not controlled by them – as many other people are. Instead, extreme athletes do what they love most – even if that happens to be something scary.

The first times you practice a new fear-coping strategy might feel unnatural or otherwise complicated to you. It's not as easy for people who are new to this skill to force themselves to 'pause, reflect and reset' right before they tumble into a panic attack as it has become for fear experts like American rock climber Lynn Hill. But she had to learn the method at some point in her life, as well – and now it is something that she does automatically. So you can do that, too. If you practice it consistently enough, there is a good chance that the emotion of fear will start feeling like a 'fly landing on your shoulder'. A small distraction from the goal you are pursuing, but not big enough to keep you from reaching it.

Afterword

...WITHIN CERTAIN BOUNDARIES

That having been said, it is also true that there are probably personal boundaries to what each human being can reach by mastering fear-coping methods. Some people are more vulnerable to stress than others, either for psychological reasons (how you are wired), or because of social processes (what you have learned through life experiences). Some people are overcome with vertigo as soon as they stand on top of the kitchen steps, while others still feel pretty relaxed when they hang onto a rock face in Yosemite. It will take the first group of people much more effort and practice than the second before they can hike on a narrow path on top of a high mountain and can actually enjoy the view.

To give a personal example: when I first started rock climbing, I suffered from extreme vertigo. After my first route in a (fairly low) gym, I came down completely pale, trembling all over, so dizzy I could hardly see and feeling physically sick. That became a pattern during my first weeks of climbing – let's say I've had times in my life where I felt better – though, for some mysterious reason, I did like the sport enough not to want to give it up now that I had discovered it. It wasn't just the mental fear of having to trust the gear, the belayer and my own muscle power that made me feel sick; much more, it was an intense physical response to being up high – a response that many beginner climbers do not experience. After a few years of climbing, however, and thanks to a lot of practicing with many of the methods described in this book, I no longer suffer from severe vertigo. I climb several times a week in a gym with a lot of joy; I typically spend my holidays on the rocks and have even come to like multi-pitching – climbing several routes above another, so that the complete ascent becomes relatively high. I still get afraid, sometimes, but I know how to control that fear, and can climb on.

But I don't dare to climb without a rope, or to jump of a cliff in a wingsuit, or to balance over a slackline hundreds of feet above the ground. And that's okay. Because even if I did have the talent to do these things successfully, it would take me years and years of practice to overcome the fear that I would face at such moments. And that, to me, is not worth all that time and energy. Although I can, on an intuitive level, imagine what a free and amazing feeling it must be to engage in those activities, I don't feel a deep longing to try them, and I feel perfectly happy not doing them. And so for me, putting in all the effort I would probably need to learn and do them without being overly afraid is simply not worth it.

Everyone has to set their own, personal boundaries for themselves. They will be defined by your current fears and wishes, and by how important you feel it is to achieve a certain dream that attracts you, but frightens you as well. In some cases, things will seem so scary and difficult that trying to do them will cost you more than it will give you in return. In other cases, it might well be worth going for it. And if you apply the methods in this book, don't be surprised if you succeed sooner than you'd expected. The best that can happen is that you make a dream come true. The worst is that you try – and adjust your goal after you find that you can't reach your initial goal. In both cases, you will have experienced transformation and growth. Because, as Mark Manson wrote, bravery is not the absence of fear. Bravery is feeling the fear, the doubt, the insecurity, and deciding that something else is more important.

SOME WORDS OF THANKS

A big thank you to all the athletes and sports coaches who were willing to spend some hours of their precious time on this book, while they looked longingly out of their windows towards the mountains – only to be disturbed by yet another question from me. I am grateful for your patience and your openness, and for your help in creating this book.

Thanks to my Dutch publisher Brandt for supporting the English publication, and to translator and fellow climbing-lover Andy Brown for his excellent editing work.

Afterword

Finally, a bow and a wave to all the readers who have contacted me over the past years to share their own stories of fear and bravery. The fact that so many of them have successfully applied the methods described in this book to start living their dreams has resulted in the Fearlessly Fearful community and platform – which has become a constant pool of inspiration and fun in my own and many others' lives. You rock.

DEFINITIONS AND TERMS THAT COME IN HANDY WHEN READING THIS BOOK

Mountaineering – an umbrella term for activities such as climbing (rock and ice) and trekking up mountains.

BASE jumping – BASE stands for Building, Antenna, Span, and Earth. BASE jumpers leap from any and all of these four fixed objects with parachutes designed specifically for rapid deployment. This sport is regarded as extremely dangerous, because of the risk of crashing against the object that BASE jumpers fly off from.

Buildering – describes the act of climbing on the outside of buildings and other artificial structures. This sport is often practiced outside legal bounds, and without a rope or other safety equipment. The word "buildering" combines the word building with the climbing term 'bouldering' (climbing low, but technically difficult routes on boulders, without ropes). If done without ropes or protection far off the ground, buildering may be dangerous.

Highlining – similar to slacklining (see below), but done at a great height. Highliners typically use safety gear, which makes their sport relatively safe.

Slacklining – the act of walking or balancing along a suspended length of flat line that is tensioned between two anchors.

Solo climbing – if a climber has climbed something 'solo' this means that there was no human belayer helping him. This act can still be relatively safe, as the climber can use a self-blocking belay device. Solo climbing should not be mistaken for free solo climbing! (See below)

Sport climbing – climbing routes on rocks or in a gym, which are secured through safety gear fixed in the wall. This sport is relatively safe.

Traditional climbing – also known as 'trad climbing'. A sport where climbers typically ascend long and steep rock faces while placing all gear required to protect against falls, removing it again when a passage is complete. This sport is considered relatively risky, because equipment material is not fixed in the wall, and, if pulled out, the climber might make long falls.

Free climbing – also called 'all-free climbing'. The terms refer to rock climbing without the assistance of devices such as pegs placed in the rock, but the climber is allowed to use ropes and belays. If a free climb is successful, it means that the climber has been able to get to the top, but not necessarily at once – falling and resting along the way are allowed. Again, this is not to be confused with free solo climbing (see below).

Free solo climbing – climbing without any form of material protection. A potential fall probably leads to death or severe injury; this sport is considered extremely dangerous.

Wingsuiting – Wingsuit flying is essentially skydiving while wearing a suit with fabric stretched between the legs and under the arms. When the arms and legs are spread, the suit acts as an airfoil, allowing the skydiver to remain airborne for much longer than a normal free fall. At the end of the flight, the wingsuiter opens a parachute in order to land.

REFERENCES

For the Introduction, I was inspired by, and have used fragments of text from, the following literature:

Bannink, F. 2017. 101 Solution-focused Questions for Help with Anxiety. W.W. Norton & Company, Inc, New York.

Bevoort, M. 2015. *Angst is voor softies.* (Dutch article on 'fear is for pussies') Grazia magazine, published 11 Mayt, pp 81-83.

Brymer, E. 2017. Adrenaline zen: what 'normal people' can learn from extreme sports. Online article on The Conversation, accessible through http://theconversation.com/adrenaline-zen-what-normal-people-can-learn-from-extreme-sports-72944

Brymer, E. 2012. BASE jumping from the Rialto: plain stupid or something else entirely? Online article on The Conversation, accessible through http://theconversation.com/base-jumping-from-the-rialto-plain-stupid-or-something-else-entirely-5875

Brymer, E., & Schweitzer, R. 2013. The Search for Freedom in Extreme Sports: A phenomenological exploration. Psychology of Sport and Exercise, 14, pp. 865-873.

Caldwell, T. 2017. Why Alex Honnold's Free Solo of El Cap Scared Me. 5 June, Outside Online.

Costa, S. 2013. See Success: How visualization leads to red pointing. Climbing Magazine, p. 23.

De Jongh, R. 2010. *Wat doet stress met ons lichaam en brein?* (original in Dutch; article on the effects of stress for our body and brain) Psychologie Magazine, May.

References

Harrer, H. 1999. The White Spider: The Classic Account of the Ascent of the Eiger. HarperCollins Publishers.

Hintum, M. van. 2017. Brein onder druk: Over stress, agressie en veerkracht. (original in Dutch; scientific book on stress, agression and resilience) SWP Publishers,

Krakauer, J. 1998. *De Ijle Lucht In: Het verslag van een huiveringwekkende Mount Everest-expeditie.* (Into Thin Air, Dutch translation) Prometheus, Amsterdam.

Kramer, F. 2015. *Motivatie.* (Dutch article on how motivation works) Flow, July. pp 125-127.

Loria, K. 2016. What the brain of a guy who climbs massive cliffs without ropes can teach us about fear. Business Insider.

Martha, C., Sanchez, X., Goma-i-Freixanet, M. 2009. Risk perception as a function of risk exposure amongst rock climbers. Psychology of Sport and Exercise, 10, pp. 193-200.

Monasterio, E., Mulder, R., Frampton, C & Mei-Dan, O. 2012. Personality characteristics of BASE jumpers. Journal of Applied Sport Psychology, 24(4), pp. 391-400.

Post, G. 2016. *Stalen zenuwen: Hoe topsporters presteren onder druk (en wat jij daarvan kunt leren).* (original in Dutch; non-fiction book on how top athletes cope with stress) Mave Publishing, Amsterdam.

Simpson, J. 1996. Touching the Void. Vintage.

Van Leeuwen, A. 2014. M*eer plezier in het klimmen: Hoe overwin ik voorklimangst.* (Dutch article on how to overcome fear of lead climbing) Hoogtelijn, 4, pp. 16-21.

Vogt Isaksen, J. The Psychology of Extreme Sports: Addicts, not Loonies.

Woodman, T., Hardy, L., Barlow, M., & Le Scanff, C. Motives for participation in prolonged engagement high-risk sports: An agentic emotion regulation perspective.

References

CHAPTER 1- ALAIN ROBERT

(Anonymous author) 2015. *Alain Robert, le spiderman français, escalade la tour Montparnasse avec le drapeau du Népal*. Online article, Le Dauphine, 30 April, accessible through http://www.ledauphine.com/france-monde/2015/04/28/alain-robert-le-spiderman-francais-se-lance-a-l-assaut-de-la-tour-montparnasse

(Anonymous author). 2015. Alain Robert: Meet the real amazing Spider-Man. Online article, Express and Star, accessible through: http://www.expressandstar.com/news/local-news/2015/11/04/alain-robert-meet-the-real-amazing-spider-man/

Official website Alain Robert: http://www.alainrobert.com/

CHAPTER 2- ALEX HONNOLD

Bagley, P. 2015. The Stepping Stone: Behind the Scenes of Alex Honnold's Half Dome Solo Ascent, Rock and Ice, 226, 16-224.

Chancellor, W. 2014. Alex Honnold. Online article, Interview Magazine, accessible: http://www.interviewmagazine.com/culture/alex-honnold#_

Chin, J. 2013. Off the Wall: Interview with Climber Alex Honnold. Online article from Jimmy Chin's blog, accessible through: http://blog.jimmychin.com/2013/07/off-the-wall-interview-with-climber-alex-honnold/

Dean, J. Not dated. His life in his hands. Online article on Men's Fitness website, accessible through: http://www.mensfitness.com/life/outdoor/his-life-in-his-hands#sthash.5V2YVxzu.dpuf

Duanemarch, D. 2015. The Heart-Stopping Climbs of Alex Honnold: The master of climbing without ropes spends his life cheating death. Online article from New York Times, accessible through: http://www.nytimes.com/2015/03/11/magazine/the-heart-stopping-climbs-of-alex-honnold.html?_r=0

Gayle, D. 2014. Who needs ropes? Fearless climber clutches fingertips to scale 2,500ft rock face that is 'as smooth as glass'. Daily Mail, 13 February.

Honnold, A., & Roberts, D. 2016. Alone on the Wall. W.W. Norton.

McCoy, S. 2015. Life or Death Climbing: Alex Honnold Q&A. Online article on GearJunkie website, accessible through: https://gearjunkie.com/interview-climber-alex-honnold-climbing-2015

CHAPTER 3 - ALEXANDER SCHULTZ

Blake, M. He really drew that out! Daredevil smashes world record for longest distance ever walked on a highline – as he tiptoes 1,230FEET. Online article in the Daily Mail, accessible through:

http://www.dailymail.co.uk/news/article-2865758/He-really-drew-Daredevil-smashes-world-record-longest-distance-walked-highline-tiptoes-1-230FEET.html#ixzz3yLxpDoIR

Strege, D. 2014. Alexander Schulz sets slacklining world record. Online article on the Grindtv website, accessible through: http://www.grindtv.com/random/alexander-schulz-sets-slacklining-world-record/#xzUgbUHeAqP2DOTT.97

One Inch Dreams website: http://www.oneinchdreams.com/en.html

CHAPTER 4 - ARNO ILGNER

Fox, A. 2013. Breathe Easier: Use these mental tricks to get through tough climbs. Online article van de website Climbing.com, accessible through: http://www.climbing.com/skills/breathe-easier-mental-tacks-to-get-through-tough-climbs/

Ilgner, A. 2006. The Rock Warrior's Way: Mental Training for Climbers. Desederate Institute.

Ilgner, A. 2009. Espresso Lessons. Desederate Institute.

Ward, M. 2010. The Warrior's Way: Arno Ilgner Discusses Fear in

Climbing. Online article op de website alpinist.com, accessible through http://www.alpinist.com/doc/web10x/wfeature-arno-ilgner-fear-climbing

Arno Ilgner's website: http://warriorsway.com/

CHAPTER 5 - CATHERINE DESTIVELLE

(Anonymous author). 2012. Interview with Catherine Destivelle. Online article on 'Bouldering Stuff' website, accessible through: https://boulderingstuff.wordpress.com/2012/05/14/interview-with-catherine-destivelle/

Arthur, C. 1998. Mother of all climbdowns: France's foremost female climber is giving up mountains to concentrate on family life. The Independent.

Catherine Destivelle's website: www.catharinedestivelle.com

CHAPTER 6 - CEDRIC DUMONT

Raspoet, E. 2015. *Cedric Dumont, de man die vliegt als een vogel* (Flemish/Dutch article about 'the man who can fly'). De Standaard Weekend, 15 April.

Spoormakers, S. 2012. Basejumper Cedric Dumont. HUMO, 13 February.

Official website of Cedric Dumont: http://www.cedricdumont.com/

CHAPTER 7 - DAN GOODWIN

Constable, B. 2014. Wallenda supported, Spider-Dan nearly killed. The Daily Herald, 11 April.

Parker, C. 2014. Dan Goodwin Sets New World Record for Longest Lead Climb. Rock and Ice Magazine, 7 March.

Dan Goodwin's websites: http://dangoodwin.co/ and http://www.tripleblack.com/

CHAPTER 8- DON MCGRATH

McGrath, D., & Elison, J. 2014. Vertical Mind: Psychological Approaches for Optimal Rock Climbing. Sharp End Publishing, Boulder Colorado.

McGrath, D., & Elison, J. 2014. Three Signs You're Afraid to Fall And How To Break Those Habits Holding You Back. Online article, published on the website Evening Sends, 30 April. URL: http://eveningsends.com/three-signs-youre-afraid-to-fall/

McGrath, D. 2015. The 5 Mindsets of Climbing: How to Train Them for High Performance Rock Climbing. E-book, accessible through: www.masterrockclimber.com

McGrath, D. 2017. The Climb. Motivational Press.

CHAPTER 9- EDURNE PASABAN

Bradley, R. 2010. Adventurers of the year 2010: The Alpinist. Edurne Pasaban. Online article on National Geographic website, accessible through: http://adventure.nationalgeographic.com/adventure/adventurers-of-the-year/edurne-pasaban-2010/

Nash, E. 2009. Edurne Pasaban: Queen of the top of the world. The Independent, 25 May.

Official Edurne Pasaban website: https://www.edurnepasaban.com/en

CHAPTER 10 - HAZEL FINDLAY

Cate (no last name mentioned). 2013. Girl Crush of the Month: Hazel Findlay. Blog on Crux Crush, 30 September.

Findlay, H. (not dated). 5 Things You Didn't Know: Hazel Findlay. Online article on Black Diamond website, accessible through: https://blackdiamondequipment.com/en/5-things-you-didnt-know-hazel-findlay.html

Mary (no last name mentioned). 2014. In it for Adventure: Interview with Hazel Findlay. Blog on Crux Crush, 5 August.

References

Rodden, B. 2012. Hazel Findlay and the next generation of climbing. Blogpost, accessible through: http://bethrodden.com/2012/11/hazel-findlay-and-the-next-generation-of-climbing/

Official Hazel Findlay website: http://hazelfindlayclimbing.com/ and her (business) Facebook page: https://www.facebook.com/hazelfindlayathlete/

CHAPTER 11 - JORG VERHOEVEN

Anonymous author. 2014. *Jorg Verhoeven levert klimprestatie van wereldformaat* (Dutch article about Verhoeven's top performance). NKBV, 10 November.

Pohl, B. 2014. INTERVIEW: Jorg Verhoeven about The Free Nose. Online article on UK Climbing website, accessible through: http://www.ukclimbing.com/news/item.php?id=69291

Verhoeven, J. 2015. *Nothin' But Sunshine. Boulderen in Colorado en de beklimming van The Nose* (Dutch article on Verhoeven's climbing experience in the US). Hoogtelijn, 2, pp. 46-49.

CHAPTER 12 - LYNN HILL

Clash, J. 2016. Climbing Legend Lynn Hill Competed Against Men - And Whipped Them! Article published on 3 January in Forbes, 'Lifestyle' section.

Hill, L., & Child, G. 2002. Climbing Free. W.W. Norton & Company Inc, New York.

Lynn Hill's website: http://lynnhillclimbing.com/

CHAPTER 13 - MARTIN FICKWEILER

Anonymous author. 2008. *Dood klimt soms met expeditie mee* (Dutch article about Fickweiler's experience with the death of a fellow climber, friend and expedition member). BN De Stem, 9 August.

Prins, M. 2014. 'Ik oefende door bruggen en kunstwerken te beklimmen.' (Dutch article about Fickweiler), National Geotraveler, 24 December.

Martin Fickweiler's website: http://blog.martinfickweiler.nl/

CHAPTER 14 - STEPH DAVIS

Davis, S. 2007. High Infatuation: A Climber's Guide to Love and Gravity. The Mountaineers Books, Seattle.

Davis, S. 2013. Learning to Fly: A Memoir of Hanging On and Letting Go. Touchstone, New York.

Website Steph Davis: http://stephdavis.co/

CHAPTER 15 - REBECCA WILLIAMS

Cate (no last name mentioned). 2015. Climbing in the Year 2030: Climbing Mentality. Blog on Crux Crush, 15 July.

Stirling, S. (not dated). Smart Climbing. Online article on Outdoor Enthousiast's Magazine, accessible through: http://sarahstirling.com/most-popular-articles/smart-climbing/

Williams, R. 2008. Psychology in Climbing: Navigating the Minefield. Online article on UK climbing website, accessible through: http://www.ukclimbing.com/articles/page.php?id=1127

Rebecca Williams' website: http://smartclimbing.co.uk/

PHOTO CREDITS

Front cover photo:

BASE jumper Steph Davis jumps of a cliff in in Moab, Utah. (Year unknown). Credits: Ian Mitchard. Front cover photo & Chapter 14 - Steph Davis

Photo Chapter 1 – Alain Robert

'Spiderman' Alain Robert reaches the top of a building. (Year unknown). Credits: Alain Robert.

Photo Chapter 2 – Alex Honnold.

Alex Honnold free solo climbs the Sentinel, 2011. Credits: Peter Mortimer.

Photo Chapter 3 – Alexander Schulz

Alexander Schulz losing balance on his highline. Credits: oneinchdreams.com

Photo Chapter 5 – Catherine Destivelle

Catherine Destivelle during an expedition. (Year unknown). Credits: René Robert.

Photo Chapter 6 – Cedric Dumont

Cedric Dumont wingsuiting over the pyramids in Gizeh, Egypt, 2015. Credits: Noah Banson.

Photo chapter 7 - Dan Goodwin

Dan Goodwin at the 87th floor of the WTC building in New York, 1983. Credits: AP Photo.

Photo chapter 9 – Edurne Pasaban

Edurne Pasaban during an ice cold expedition. (Year unknown).

Credits: Edurne Pasaban.

Photo chapter 10 – Jorg Verhoeven

Jorg Verhoeven during his ascent of The Nose, 2014. Credits: Jon Glassberg.

Photo chapter 11 – Hazel Findlay

Hazel Findlay free solo climbs in Oman. Credits: Jimmy Chin.

Photo chapter 12 – Lynn Hill

Lynn Hill climbs the last part of The Nose, El Capitan, 1993. Credits: John Bachar.

Photo chapter 13 – Martin Fickweiler

Self-portrait on Baffin Island, 2013. Credits: Martin Fickweiler.

ABOUT THE AUTHOR

Roanne van Voorst is an anthropologist, public speaker and author of fiction and non-fiction. She obtained her PhD (with honors) for research on risk behavior, and has continued to do research on the themes of fear and risk behavior in settings all over the world, from Inuit villages to the slums of Jakarta, Indonesia. Her current research investigates the risk experiences and fear management strategies of soldiers, humanitarians and refugees working or living in conflict settings.

Roanne has developed and offers on-and offline courses, through which she helps people all over the world to overcome their fears and live their bravest live into 'and live more adventurous and intentional lives with scientifically-proven effective methods.

For more information:

www.fearlesslyfearful.com

www.roannevanvoorst.com

Printed in Great Britain
by Amazon